NEXT IS NOW!

Dealing with the Overdose of Doubt

Dr. Jennifer Bishop

Copyright © 2023 – Dr. Jennifer Bishop

All rights reserved. No part of this book may be used or reproduced in any manner whatsoever without written permission except in the case of brief quotations embodied in critical articles or reviews.

Thank you for buying an authorized edition of this book and for complying with copyright laws by not reproducing, scanning, or distributing any part of it in any form without permission. You are supporting writers and their hard work by doing this.

JB

Published in the USA by BishopSpeaks Publishing

First Printing Edition, 2023

TABLE OF CONTENTS

Introduction 1
Why I Wrote this Book? 3
What We'll Explore 4
Next is Now! Dealing With the Overdose of Doubt 8

Chapter 1 – Iconic Leadership: An Overview 9
Imposter Syndrome & Leadership Over the Years 10

Chapter 2 – Understanding Self-Doubt and Imposter Syndrome 14
Self-Doubt vs. Imposter Syndrome 16
Why Self-Doubt & Imposter Syndrome Creep In.. 19
How Self-Doubt & Imposter Syndrome Manifest 22

Chapter 3 – Types of Imposter Syndrome 25
The Various Faces of Imposter Syndrome 26
Who Will Likely Experience Imposter Syndrome 29
How to Identify Your Imposter Syndrome 32

Chapter 4 – Recognizing the Signs of Self-Doubt and Imposter Syndrome 35
Common Signs & Symptoms 37
The Effects of the Symptoms 43
Seeking Help 45

Chapter 5 – Overcoming Self-Doubt and Imposter Syndrome 49
Strategies to Overcome Imposter Syndrome 50
When All Else Fails 55
The Proof is in the Pudding 57

Chapter 6 – Dismantling the Inner Critic 61
Looking Toward Limiting Self-Beliefs 63
Developing a Growth Mindset 66
Leveraging Personal Strengths & Values 69
Practicing Self-Care 71

Chapter 7 – Leadership Styles and Traits for Modern Leaders 74
Effective Leadership Styles 75
Modeling Those Who Have Gone Before Us 79

Chapter 8 – Communication Skills for Leaders 82
Why Communication is Key 83
How to Begin Improving Communication Skills 86

Understanding Listening & Communicating Styles 88
Learning From Notable Communicators 91

Chapter 9 – Navigating Bias and Discrimination 94
It's (NOT) All in Your Head 96
How This Impacts Our Experiences 100
Recognizing Toxicity & Calling It Out 103

Chapter 10 – Building Self-Confidence 110
Milestones That Matter 111
Stepping Out of Your Comfort Zone 114
Why You Should Shift Your Perspective 114
How to Reframe Your POV 117

Chapter 11 – The Power of Vulnerability 120
Leave No Stone Unturned 122
Learning How to Embrace Vulnerability 124
Vulnerable Leaders in Spotlight 125

Chapter 12 – Allowing Intuition to Be
Your Guide in the Workplace 128
How Self-Doubt Impacts Our Careers 129
Dealing with Self-Doubt in the Workplace 131
Knowing Who Your Allies Are 133

Chapter 13 – Overcoming Self-Doubt and Imposter Syndrome in Personal Relationships 137
Imposter Syndrome in the Personal Realm 139
Coming Back to Those Who Care 142
The Reality of Our Global Society 145

Chapter 14 – Sustaining Confidence Over Time 148
Keeping Up Confidence in the Long Run 149
Growing & Nurturing Your Network 152
Driving Adaptability 154
Continuing Your Growth 155

Conclusion: Call to Action 157
References & Citations 160

INTRODUCTION

"I always did something I was a little not ready to do. I think that's how you grow. When there's that moment of 'Wow, I'm not really sure I can do this,' and you push through those moments, that's when you have a breakthrough."

~ Marissa Mayer (Co-Founder, Lumi Labs)

The prevalence of women in leadership positions has increased in recent years, marking significant progress toward gender equality. However, despite these advancements, women continue to grapple with self-doubt and imposter syndrome in today's society. This is in spite of the fact that women's representation in leadership positions has witnessed a positive trend across various fields, including politics, business, and academia. Many countries have made strides in narrowing the gender gap in leadership, with women assuming prominent roles as CEOs, heads of state, and high-ranking officials.

Nonetheless, women's representation remains disproportionately low compared to their male counterparts, and there are several reasons for this fact. First, societal norms, biases, and structural barriers continue to hinder women's ascent to leadership positions, leading to a lack of diverse perspectives and a missed opportunity for inclusive decision-making. Second, the issues associated with self-doubt and imposter syndrome can stand as barriers to pursuing leadership roles.

Women leaders often face an internal struggle with self-doubt, questioning their abilities and qualifications despite their accomplishments. This self-doubt can stem from various factors, including societal expectations, stereotypes, and the lack of female role models in leadership positions. Women may internalize societal messages that undermine their confidence, perpetuating a cycle of self-doubt and hesitancy to seize opportunities. Additionally, the threat of stereotyping can further contribute to their self-doubt, as women may fear confirming negative stereotypes about their competence in leadership roles.

This, in itself, can tighten the grip of imposter syndrome, which is characterized by persistent feelings of inadequacy and fear of being exposed as a fraud. This is an incredibly common experience among women in leadership. Despite their accomplishments and qualifications, women may attribute their success to luck or external factors, downplaying their own capabilities. Imposter syndrome undermines women's confidence, causing them to question their abilities and often leading to self-sabotage. The fear of being discovered as an imposter can also discourage women from taking on new challenges or pursuing higher positions, perpetuating the gender disparity in leadership.

Why I Wrote this Book?

In my first book, *Now Get Up and Go Be Great*™, I focused on giving inspirational and affirming thoughts on how one could get up after being knocked down. And I didn't want them to merely get up—no, I wanted them to do it now, during that moment of helplessness. I wanted them to recognize that they could get up and go be great! I wanted to encourage them to realize that they may have had to momentarily slow down, but they did not have permission to stay down. Yet, as a leader, I understand that the struggles faced can be paralyzing, and it is critical to explore what can keep and has kept us from getting up and going to be great.

Two things I know personally are self-doubt and imposter syndrome. Everyone has a healthy dose of anxiety and fear, but the problem occurs when a person overdoses on it. When uncertainties linger in our lives instead of confidence in our decisions to move forward, many of us become personally and professionally paralyzed.

These two barriers can be the most crippling challenges to not only aspiring leaders but people already in leadership positions who are aspiring for higher levels. But it's not enough to just talk about the problem—we must explore solutions. Empowering leaders and creating supportive environments are both within our grasp when we confront the underlying issues of self-doubt and imposter syndrome.

This means promoting diverse role models, offering mentorship and support networks, and even challenging gender sterrotypes. Organizations have a role to play, too - by implementing policies and practices that value and recognize significant contributions. Together, we can create a culture of inclusivity and empowerment.

Keep in mind that it's not just up to organizations. Leaders themselves must take charge of our development, building resilience and challenging our own self-limiting beliefs. By coming together and facing these challenges head-on, we can unlock the full potential of modern-day leaders. And in doing so, we'll foster equality and drive positive change across all sectors.

By actively addressing these challenges that come with self-doubt and fostering an inclusive and supportive environment, society can empower aspiring leaders to overcome self-doubt and fulfill their potential.

What We'll Explore

My goal with this book is to explore the prevalence of imposter syndrome amongst people in leadership roles - delving into the factors contributing to self-doubt and imposter syndrome. I'll highlight the importance of addressing these challenges to empower those in leadership.

INTRODUCTION

We will explore the historical context of imposter syndrome in leadership, discussing the iconic leaders that have come before us in a number of fields.

As we dive into Chapter 2, we will define self-doubt and imposter syndrome, explaining their origins and impacts, and providing examples of how these feelings can manifest in different aspects of our lives. You will gain a deep understanding of the psychological dynamics behind self-doubt and imposter syndrome.

From there, we'll explore the different types of imposter syndrome, such as perfectionism, the expert, the soloist, and others. By helping you identify which type of imposter syndrome you may be experiencing, the book offers personalized insights and strategies for overcoming specific manifestations of imposter syndrome.

Not only this, but you'll also learn to identify the common symptoms of self-doubt and imposter syndrome and understand how these symptoms can be detrimental to your personal and professional life. This is all before we begin unpacking strategies for overcoming self-doubt and imposter syndrome, such as mindfulness and positive self-talk, among many others.

What's more, real-life stories of individuals who jae successfully overcome these challenges offer inspiration and motivation.

As you begin exploring ways to build inner confidence, you'll most likely find that there are a few areas that are ripe for improvement that have now become obvious to you. This will include recognizing and overcoming limiting beliefs and self-doubt, developing a growth mindset, identifying and leveraging personal strengths and values, and practicing self-care and self-compassion.

Ultimately, you'll be shown various leadership styles and traits that are effective for modern-day leaders. We'll take a deep dive into the importance of communication skills in leadership before discussing how to navigating the subject of bias and discrimination that leaders – and their team members - may encounter.

Our final chapters will see us walking through tips for building self confidence, setting achievable goals, practicing self-care, celebrating successes, and shifting our mindset to overcome imposter syndrome. You'll discover how embracing vulnerability can help overcome imposter syndrome and how self-doubt and imposter syndrome can affect personal relationships.

At the end of it all, I'll provide you with strategies for maintaining confidence during challenging times and tips on how to nurture supportive networks, build resilience, and adapt to change.

INTRODUCTION

So, are you ready to become the leader that you know you're capable of becoming? Are you ready to stop allowing self-doubt and imposter syndrome from getting you to your next? If so, the journey is about to begin because your **Next is Now!**

DR. JENNIFER BISHOP

Next is Now! Dealing With the Overdose of Doubt.

CHAPTER 1
ICONIC LEADERSHIP: AN OVERVIEW

The landscape of leadership around the world today is characterized by progress and persistent challenges. While we have made significant strides in redefining leadership roles, some antiquated modalities persist. Added to this is the fact that countless leaders bear the weight of an ongoing struggle with imposter syndrome and self-doubt.

Even though just as many leaders have created environments in which both they and their teams can flourish—and truly be pioneers in their own rights—there is still a crippling anxiety that looms large. This often has catastrophic results because leadership, as a force for positive transformation, must be rooted in leading by example. Of course, leading by example becomes a heavily convoluted tight rope act when one is battling with the echoes of their own inner critic. This, in turn, inhibits leaders from allowing themselves and others to learn from adversity and transcend traditional authoritarian modalities.

This is something that we must address because leadership, after all, is about inspiring collective action and driving change.

To address these hurdles, a comprehensive strategy must emerge—one that engages individuals, institutions, and policymakers. Ultimately, the path forward demands a departure from outdated paradigms. Authoritarian modalities, often rooted in the past, must be replaced with collaborative, adaptive leadership. Leading by example must become the cornerstone, where authenticity and accountability underpin every action. Learning from adversity, rather than being undermined by it, must set the stage for growth and resilience to burst onto the scene.

In essence, leadership is about creating a space where individuals, irrespective of their background, can thrive and contribute. It is about fostering an environment where every voice is heard and each || is valued.

As we progress, we must remember that leadership is a dynamic, evolving endeavor—one that is greatly influenced by societal shifts and collective aspirations. By recognizing the broader context and embracing a holistic perspective, we can lay the foundation for a more inclusive and impactful leadership landscape.

So, let us begin our unpacking of imposter syndrome and self-doubt.

Imposter Syndrome & Leadership Over the Years

Imposter syndrome is a phenomenon where individuals doubt their accomplishments and fear being exposed as frauds. It transcends gender, age, and occupation—quietly creeping up on those it wishes to sink its claws into. Throughout history, even the most accomplished individuals have wrestled with these feelings, and their journeys offer valuable lessons for leaders across the spectrum. The following notable figures, among many others, have openly shared their struggles with imposter syndrome, serving as inspirations for overcoming self-doubt and achieving greatness.

- **Harriet Tubman**, the fearless American abolitionist and social activist renowned for her role in the Underground Railroad, battled imposter syndrome as she led countless enslaved individuals to freedom. Despite her extraordinary bravery, Tubman often questioned her leadership abilities, demonstrating that imposter syndrome can affect even the most heroic figures.

- Then there is none other than **Serena Williams**—widely regarded as one of the greatest tennis players of all time. She has faced her share of self-doubt and imposter syndrome. Despite her numerous Grand Slam titles and unmatched athleticism, Williams has admitted to struggling with feelings of not being good enough. Through determination and resilience, she has become an iconic figure of perseverance for aspiring athletes and leaders.

- **U.S. Supreme Court Justice Sonia Sotomayor** has also openly shared her struggles with imposter syndrome, particularly as they relate to her early career. Her ascent to the highest court in the land serves as a powerful testament to overcoming self-doubt and embracing one's capabilities.

- **Maya Angelou**, the iconic poet and civil rights activist, once famously revealed feeling like a fraud despite her literary genius and profound impact on society. As a renowned poet, author, and civil rights activist, she is revered for her wisdom and eloquence. However, despite all of this, she too battled with imposter syndrome throughout her life. Despite her immense talent and contributions to the world, Angelou often felt undeserving of her success. You wouldn't know it by the way that she often wrote and spoke of the beauty and strength of being a woman. Through her poetry and writings, she encouraged others to confront their insecurities and find their voices even when she felt like hers was wavering.

- Renowned actress, comedian, and producer **Tina Fey** has also humorously addressed imposter syndrome throughout her career. Her candid discussions remind us that even those who bring joy to millions can grapple with self-doubt.

Ultimately, the stories of these remarkable women remind us that imposter syndrome is a shared human experience. They teach us that doubts and insecurities can coexist with incredible achievements. However, these doubts do not have to define us. Each figure has demonstrated the capacity to transcend imposter syndrome—proving that with determination, self-awareness, and support, anyone can rise above self-doubt to become a confident and impactful leader.

*

In the upcoming chapters, we'll begin unpacking what the terms "imposter syndrome" and "self-doubt" actually mean within the context of leadership. Not only that, but we'll continue exploring the narrative of world-renowned leaders who have suffered from the same effects. When all is said and done, you'll see just how prevalent this all is and be assured that you are not alone. Let's move on.

CHAPTER 2

UNDERSTANDING SELF-DOUBT AND IMPOSTER SYNDROME

Understanding self-doubt and imposter syndrome is crucial for leaders in the modern workplace. These feelings can have a significant impact on leadership effectiveness, career advancement, and overall well-being. By delving into the nature of self-doubt and imposter syndrome, leaders can gain valuable insights into their own experiences and develop strategies to overcome these challenges.

Before we can unpack the means by which we'll tackle self-doubt and imposter syndrome, we need to fully understand what these phenomena are. Self-doubt refers to a lack of confidence or belief in one's abilities, while imposter syndrome is characterized by persistent feelings of inadequacy and the fear of being exposed as a fraud. Both phenomena can occur despite evidence of one's competence and achievements. These two concepts often intertwine, with self-doubt often fueling imposter syndrome.

In the workplace, leaders may experience self-doubt and imposter syndrome due to various factors. From lack of representation to preconceived notions about your own abilities, even the mindset—or belief systems—that you were raised with can play a part. If you're unaware of how that might play out in terms of imposter syndrome, you could find yourself in a situation where the lack of representation makes you feel as though you're in a space that you're not meant to be in. The issue with this is that as time goes by and stress sets in, even the most confident individual can begin believing these sentiments. This, in turn, can make it more challenging for them to assert their leadership and navigate career progression.

Self-doubt and imposter syndrome can hinder the development of effective leadership skills. Leaders who doubt themselves may hesitate to make decisions, second-guess their choices, or avoid taking risks. This can impede their ability to inspire and guide their teams, impacting overall team performance and organizational success. It can also limit their willingness to step into leadership roles and pursue career advancement opportunities.

However, the impact of self-doubt and imposter syndrome extends beyond leadership abilities. These feelings can negatively affect mental and emotional well-being, leading to chronic stress, anxiety, and burnout. The constant fear of being exposed as an imposter can create relentless pressure to prove oneself, eroding self-confidence and satisfaction in one's accomplishments. While working hard to be the best version of oneself is commendable, doing it because of a constant feeling of inferiority or inadequacy is unfathomably detrimental.

Recognizing and understanding self-doubt and imposter syndrome is the first step toward overcoming these challenges. Leaders can cultivate self-awareness by identifying the triggers and patterns of their self-doubt and imposter syndrome. They can challenge negative self-perceptions by reframing thoughts and embracing a growth mindset. Seeking support through mentorship, coaching, or peer networks can also provide invaluable guidance and encouragement. But that is only just the beginning of the road to recovery. Addressing self-doubt and imposter syndrome requires a commitment to self-care and self-compassion. And, let's face it, prioritizing your well-being and practicing stress management techniques can feel practically impossible when you're drowning in the depths of shaky mental health and a poor self-image.

Thankfully, there are tools that you can use to ensure that the effects of self-doubt and imposter syndrome are minimized and, in many cases, completely eradicated. Before I provide you with these practical tools, it's imperative that we explore the interchangeable nature of these terms.

Self-Doubt vs. Imposter Syndrome

Self-doubt and imposter syndrome are two interconnected concepts that often go hand in hand, yet they have distinct characteristics and origins.

Self-doubt can be understood as a lack of confidence or belief in one's abilities, judgment, or worth. It is a common human experience that can arise in various areas of life, including personal relationships and work. Self-doubt may stem from past failures, external criticisms, comparison to others, or internal insecurities. It often manifests as a constant questioning of oneself, a fear of making mistakes, or a persistent feeling of not being good enough. Self-doubt can undermine our confidence and hinder our ability to take risks and pursue opportunities. Imagine living in a world where every thought you think is run through two gates in your mind. The first is the normal process of deliberation, and the second is only there as an opportunity to sow doubt. This is what many people who live with self-doubt have to contend with on a daily basis.

On the other hand, imposter syndrome is a specific psychological phenomenon characterized by an internalized fear of being exposed as a fraud despite evidence of one's competence or accomplishments. Individuals experiencing imposter syndrome believe that their achievements are a result of luck or deception rather than their own abilities and hard work. They often attribute their successes to external factors or dismiss them as mere flukes. The hallmark difference between self-doubt and imposter syndrome is that imposter syndrome is accompanied by a persistent fear of being discovered as an imposter.

With imposter syndrome, the focus is placed externally, which feels as though it is something we cannot control. This can lead to anxiety and a constant striving for perfection. It can also lead to self-sabotage, and this is something that people seldom talk about. It's all too easy to skate across the surface meaning of imposter syndrome and for it to seem somewhat harmless, but when you actually dig a little deeper, you get to see how sinister of a force this can actually be in a leader's life. Self-sabotage can be categorized as a pattern of thoughts that lead to behaviors that hold us back from achieving our full potential. In other words, imposter syndrome tells us that we're not good enough to be where we are, and we engage in self-sabotaging behaviors to fulfill this idea. This, in itself, is a form of self-fulfilling prophecy, and it is incredibly dangerous because of the fact that it perpetuates a belief that is rooted in falsehoods.

This is why understanding the difference between these two phenomena is so important. While self-doubt and imposter syndrome share some similarities, such as the undermining of confidence and feelings of inadequacy, imposter syndrome is a specific manifestation of self-doubt with distinct features. Imposter syndrome tends to be more pervasive and deeply ingrained, affecting individuals across various areas of their lives and persisting even in the face of external validation and evidence of competence. Self-doubt, on the other hand, may be more situational and fluctuate depending on specific circumstances.

So, why do people get these terms mixed up?

Well, the interchangeability of the terms "self-doubt" and "imposter syndrome" can be attributed to several factors. First, imposter syndrome often arises from underlying self-doubt. As a result, the two concepts become intertwined—with imposter syndrome being a manifestation of self-doubt in a specific context. Additionally, self-doubt and imposter syndrome often coexist and reinforce each other. Individuals who experience self-doubt may be more prone to developing imposter syndrome as they attribute their achievements to external factors or luck, thus fueling their self-doubt and perpetuating the belief that they are not truly deserving of their accomplishments.

At the end of the day, it is important to recognize that while self-doubt and imposter syndrome are interconnected, they are not synonymous with one another. While imposter syndrome can't exist without some semblance of self-doubt, self-doubt can exist without manifesting into imposter syndrome.

The real question is how do either of these issues begin creeping in?

Why Self-Doubt & Imposter Syndrome Creep In

Feelings of self-doubt and imposter syndrome can arise from a variety of factors, including personal experiences, societal expectations, and internal beliefs. Understanding the roots of these feelings is crucial in addressing and overcoming them.

One major contributing factor to self-doubt and imposter syndrome is past experiences of failure or criticism. Negative feedback or setbacks can erode our confidence and create self-doubt, making us question our abilities and worth. This requires a mindset change. Without being of the firm belief that setbacks lead to greater accomplishments and that "failure" is a necessary part of one's growth, all past obstacles will seem like evidence of inadequacy. Add to that the pressures of leadership among a modern-day workforce, and you've got a recipe for disaster on your hands.

If you experience any of this and you also have internal beliefs or perfectionistic tendencies to deal with, you are going to find it exceedingly difficult to navigate challenges, thus compounding your sense of self-doubt.

Holding unrealistic standards for ourselves and fearing any deviation from perfection can fuel feelings of lack and the fear of being exposed as a fraud.

The fear of failure or making mistakes can further intensify these feelings, leading to a constant need for validation and an aversion to taking risks. This is like death to the leadership spirit because, as a leader, people will look to you for validation of their actions and performance. When there is no one above you to validate your feelings and actions, you might be tempted to look for it among your team. When this begins happening, you might seem weak in the eyes of your team and they will lose their trust in your ability to lead them. While no one is saying that you need to be a round-the-clock stoic, you need to understand that—despite your human nature—a leadership role will demand something completely different from you. In fact, every role in your life will come with its own set of requirements. In the case of leadership, leaning on your team and empowering them in their roles will not be the equivalent of relying on your team for validation of your role or leadership style. The latter is, of course, detrimental to both you and your team.

The impact of self-doubt and imposter syndrome on individuals can be profound. It can limit personal growth and hinder professional development. When individuals doubt their abilities and worth, they may hesitate to pursue opportunities or take on challenges, thus holding themselves back from reaching their full potential. This can result in missed opportunities for advancement and personal fulfillment. Furthermore, it can result in missed opportunities for the organization as a whole.

Another issue that people seldom talk about is the fact that constantly spiraling down the rabbit hole of imposter syndrome can have deep interpersonal consequences. While we'll dig deeper into this in a later chapter, it's important to note that individuals experiencing these feelings may struggle with forming and maintaining relationships, fearing that others will discover their perceived inadequacies. This can lead to social isolation and hinder meaningful connections. In a professional context, addressing these notions can be the difference between healthy relationships with your team members and codependence (or even authoritarian) attachments in the workplace—neither of which are healthy. This will only hinder collaboration and effective leadership, thus limiting diverse perspectives and contributions. When that happens, team dynamics will be hampered and you will have effectively shot organizational success in the proverbial foot.

Recognizing the impact of self-doubt and imposter syndrome is the first step in addressing these challenges. By understanding the underlying causes and the ways in which they manifest, you can develop strategies to challenge negative beliefs, build self-confidence, and cultivate a healthier mindset.

How Self-Doubt & Imposter Syndrome Manifest

As mentioned, self-doubt and imposter syndrome can manifest in various areas of our lives—affecting our personal relationships, academic pursuits, professional endeavors, and even our self-image. By examining specific examples, we can gain a deeper understanding of how these feelings can impact different aspects of our existence.

In personal relationships, self-doubt and imposter syndrome can undermine our ability to form and maintain connections. For example, individuals may question their worthiness of love and affection, leading them to doubt their partner's feelings and constantly seek reassurance. This constant need for validation can strain relationships and create a cycle of insecurity and doubt. What's more, this can become a form of self-fulfilling prophecy just as we looked at earlier. The idea of being unlovable, imperfect, or broken in some way is rooted in the idea that other people are perfect. We believe that perfection is attainable and that we, therefore, must be inherently "bad" or unworthy.

This can ripple into academic settings, where self-doubt and imposter syndrome can hinder learning and achievement. Students experiencing these feelings may downplay their accomplishments and attribute their successes to luck or easy tasks, rather than recognizing their own competence. This self-devaluation can lead to a lack of motivation and it isn't just students in academia that face this issue. For anyone who is on a mission to learn and grow, setbacks of any kind can lead to imposter syndrome if one is not confident in their own abilities.

For leaders who are actively engaged in the pursuit of lifelong learning, this can be a massive stumbling block.

In the professional realm, self-doubt and imposter syndrome can significantly impact career advancement and satisfaction. As discussed in Chapter 1, even successful leaders may experience a persistent fear of being exposed as inadequate or undeserving of their position. This fear can undermine their confidence, hinder decision-making processes, and create a reluctance to assert their authority. Consequently, imposter syndrome can limit a leader's effectiveness and impact.

This is why nipping imposter syndrome in the bud is of such importance. If it doesn't manage to push you out of your leadership role, it will have you stagnating in areas where you could be flourishing. As you sink deeper into a pattern of constantly comparing yourself to other leaders, you'll find yourself grappling with a diminished sense of self-worth—an issue that could be long-lasting in nature if not quickly addressed. This self-comparison can perpetuate and intensify imposter syndrome, as you start to truly believe you don't measure up to societal standards or the achievements of your peers.

What's worse is that all of this will rob you of your voice because you won't just feel as though your abilities are limited but that your thoughts and opinions are of poor quality as well. For leaders, this means losing the ability to advocate for themselves and set boundaries. Asserting your needs and preferences as the "head honcho" in your workplace will become impossible because of this unwarranted fear of rejection or criticism. If your business relies on innovation and creativity, which most do, this is not going to work out in anyone's best interests. Being a leader who cannot share their ideas for fear of being judged or dismissed will create an internal reluctance to rise to new challenges, which can stifle originality and prevent the development of new and valuable contributions.

To make matters worse, the more you try to push any of this under the rug, the more it will rise to the surface.

*

With a deeper understanding of self-doubt and imposter syndrome—both how they differ and how they're similar—we can begin our exploration of the types of imposter syndrome. Removing the veil of uncertainty will drastically reduce the apprehension and fear currently revolving around these issues in your life. Armed with this knowledge, you'll be able to lead a more fulfilling life and have a more elevated experience in your career. So, what are we waiting for?

CHAPTER 3
TYPES OF IMPOSTER SYNDROME

As mentioned in our last chapter, understanding the various types of imposter syndrome is essential to unpack the complexities of this phenomenon. Each type encompasses distinct characteristics, thought patterns, and emotional experiences that contribute to an individual's perception of themselves as imposters. By exploring these types, we can gain valuable insights into the underlying dynamics that drive imposter syndrome and develop targeted strategies to overcome its impact.

Through an in-depth exploration of the different types, I hope to provide you with a comprehensive understanding of the elaborate nature of the various types of imposter syndrome. Not only that, but this chapter will set the tone for our future examination of how imposter syndrome can manifest across different domains of life, including education, work, relationships, and personal pursuits. Remember, while we will touch on these topics throughout other chapters, we will have dedicated chapters in which we can dive deeper into each concept. By exploring these real-life scenarios, you'll be able to identify the common patterns and triggers associated with imposter syndrome. You'll also be able to use practical tools and techniques to help yourself overcome its grasp. So, without further ado, let's dig deeper into the many masks or faces that imposter syndrome tends to manifest and how you can identify your own experience with the syndrome.

The Various Faces of Imposter Syndrome

Understanding the different types of imposter syndrome is essential for individuals seeking to recognize and overcome these self-limiting beliefs.

The first, and quite possibly most obvious of them all, is **the perfectionist**. This type of imposter syndrome is characterized by the relentless pursuit of flawlessness. Perfectionists set exceedingly high standards for themselves and feel inadequate when they fall short—often dismissing their achievements as not good enough. They are overly critical of their own work and may procrastinate due to fear of not meeting their own impossibly high expectations.

Second, we have **the expert**. Individuals with the expert type of imposter syndrome constantly seek more knowledge and feel compelled to know everything before taking action. They believe they need to be an authority in their field, leaving little room for mistakes or learning from experience. This mindset can hinder their progress as they are hesitant to embrace new challenges or step outside of their comfort zone until they feel they have complete mastery. The major issue with this is that by the time someone feels that they have "mastered" a subject, it might be irrelevant. They fail to see the relevance that so-called on-the-job learning has.

The third is **the soloist,** and this type reflects a reluctance to ask for help or seek support. These individuals believe they must accomplish everything on their own to prove their worth. They fear that asking for assistance will expose their perceived incompetence. As a result, they may feel overwhelmed and isolated because they carry the weight of these responsibilities without seeking the collaboration and support that could enhance their outcomes.

Next is the **natural genius** or **intellectual**. Those who experience this type of imposter syndrome have an internalized expectation that they should effortlessly excel in all areas. They believe that if they struggle or need to put in the effort, it signifies a lack of inherent talent or intelligence. These individuals may avoid challenges that could potentially reveal their limitations, thus leading to stagnation in their personal and professional growth. This is closely linked to what is known as a fixed mindset because those with a fixed mindset think talent is inherent. The main flaw in this line of thinking revolves around the term "inherent talent." First and foremost, there is really no such thing as inherent talent. Talent can be honed and refined. More often than not, areas in which we are "talented" are simply areas that we take a liking to and spend a lot of time focusing on.

Finally, we have **the superwoman,** or **superman,** and this form of imposter syndrome is characterized by an intense drive to excel in all aspects of life simultaneously. If you feel like you have to be the best at work as well as in relationships and with regard to personal goals, that's perfectly normal. However, expecting to be the best in all of these areas all at once is going to drive you to insanity. You will place immense pressure on yourself to maintain a high level of achievement in every domain. If you're doing this and neglecting your own well-being in the process, you need to reassess whether what you're hoping to achieve is worth the damage you're doing. Anyone who experiences this type of imposter syndrome may struggle with balancing multiple responsibilities and feel like they are falling short despite their accomplishments.

It's important to note that individuals can experience a combination of these imposter syndrome types as well as other variations that may not fit neatly into these categories. The key is to recognize the common underlying themes and thought patterns associated with imposter syndrome, which can help you identify and address these feelings in yourself and others. Understanding the different types of imposter syndrome is essential because it allows you to recognize that your experiences are not uncommon or unique. Feeling as though you're experiencing something completely uncommon can make you feel isolated, and, in some cases, you might question your mental stability.

A deepened understanding, on the other hand, provides a framework for self-reflection and encourages you to challenge the unrealistic expectations you impose upon yourself. Plus, every road to recovery is paved with understanding. For the most part, we wouldn't walk into a doctor's office, let them run random tests on us in complete silence, and then allow them to administer a treatment without running it past us or explaining the nature of our condition to us. We, as individuals and leaders in our own rights, have a warranted desire to know more about what is affecting us and why. If we didn't, none of you would be reading this book today.

Understanding is, therefore, the key that unlocks the door to personal and professional growth. Other than understanding the type of imposter syndrome that you're likely facing, you might be wondering who is more likely to experience imposter syndrome at some point in their lives. That's a very valid inquiry and one that I intend to shed light on now.

Who Will Likely Experience Imposter Syndrome

Imposter syndrome can affect individuals from all walks of life, but certain groups of people may be more susceptible to experiencing these feelings in adulthood. While imposter syndrome can impact anyone, several factors contribute to its prevalence among certain individuals. High achievers, for example, might be the most at risk. As individuals who have a track record of significant achievements, it might become an exceptionally difficult task to keep up with themselves, thus making them prone to imposter syndrome. The more success they attain, the more they may question their abilities and fear being exposed as a fraud. High achievers set high standards for themselves and can struggle to internalize their accomplishments, attributing them to external factors rather than recognizing their own capabilities.

Of course, perfectionists are next in line to the throne of the ultimate imposter syndrome sufferer. Perfectionism and imposter syndrome are like two peas in a pod. Perfectionists have an unrelenting desire to achieve flawlessness in every aspect of their lives. They set unrealistic expectations for themselves and fear making mistakes or falling short. Perfectionists tend to be highly self-critical, dismissing their accomplishments as not meeting their impossibly high standards, leading to feelings of inadequacy.

After them, individuals in transition—or those experiencing significant life changes or transitioning into new roles—may be more prone to imposter syndrome. If you're starting a new job, pursuing higher education, becoming a parent, or changing careers, this transitionary period and the uncertainty that it brings with it can trigger self-doubt and feelings of being an imposter. The fear of not measuring up to the expectations associated with these transitions can further amplify imposter syndrome. The common thread with these groups of people, of course, is the fallout between expectation and reality or having incredibly unrealistic expectations of oneself.

This can have a doubled effect on our next group of individuals who are likely to experience imposter syndrome: minorities and underrepresented groups. People from minority or underrepresented groups—such as racial or ethnic minorities, women in male-dominated fields, or individuals from marginalized communities—often face societal stereotypes and biases that contribute to imposter syndrome. The lack of representation and the pressure to overcome stereotypes can exacerbate feelings of self-doubt and the fear of not belonging. While the stereotypical "mean girl" and "brutish jock" mentality that seemed to seep into workspaces in previous generations seems to be showing signs of letting up, there are still catty comments and snide remarks that one might have to deal with. Thankfully, company policies, amended constitutional rights, and revamped HR teams are always waiting in the wings to tackle such issues. However, that doesn't make them any less challenging to deal with. Individuals can still be quite cutthroat and competitive, which, whether you're part of an underrepresented group or not, has its own set of obstacles.

At the end of the day, individuals in industries or environments that are characterized by intense competition, comparison, or high-performance expectations can breed imposter syndrome. In fields where success is often measured against others, individuals may constantly compare themselves to their peers and doubt their own abilities. This can be particularly prevalent in creative industries, academia, or highly competitive workplaces.

Equally intense are fields that can be categorized as those belonging to highly skilled professionals. Individuals who possess exceptional talents or skills in a particular area may feel like they are not deserving of recognition or believe that their accomplishments are solely due to their natural talents rather than their hard work and dedication. The fear of being exposed as a fraud despite their exceptional abilities can contribute to imposter syndrome.

Finally, we have individuals with a history of negative feedback or rejection. For many people who begin unpacking the various types of imposter syndrome, this particular type seems to make the most sense. This is mainly due to the fact that there is at least some evidence of past difficulties that might warrant certain levels of self-doubt. Past experiences of criticism, negative feedback, or rejection can shape imposter syndrome. Individuals who have faced setbacks or harsh evaluations may internalize these experiences, doubting their abilities and feeling like they do not deserve success. Because these people might feel like their imposter syndrome is warranted, it might be even harder for them to break themselves of the idea that they're imposters. Previous failures can perpetuate imposter syndrome and make individuals question their competence even in the face of new achievements.

You'll likely have picked up on one or more themes that you might have previously experienced or are currently experiencing. However, to truly identify your imposter syndrome, there are a few steps you can take.

How to Identify Your Imposter Syndrome

According to an article in the Massachusetts Institute of Technology's *MIT Sloan Management Review*, identifying whether or not you're truly experiencing imposter syndrome is the first step to remedying the issues that may arise [1]. Of course, this can be easier said than done for high achievers such as leaders in high-performance settings. Nonetheless, by recognizing the specific characteristics and thought patterns associated with their imposter syndrome, individuals can develop strategies tailored to their unique challenges.

    The very first step that I recommend is reflecting on your thoughts and feelings. When you take time to reflect on your thoughts and emotions surrounding your accomplishments and abilities, you can trace what thoughts your self-doubt is linked to. Notice if you tend to set unreasonably high standards for yourself, fear being exposed as a fraud, or struggle with asking for help. More importantly, take note of the situations in which you find one or all three of that trifecta cropping up. Self-awareness is key in identifying the specific patterns and beliefs contributing to your imposter syndrome. Do you notice any common themes? If not, it's time to start taking note of them. Journal these themes and the moments when your imposter syndrome is often the loudest.

    When you familiarize yourself with the common types of imposter syndrome, such as those we looked at earlier, you'll be able to consider which traits resonate with your experiences and behaviors. Understanding the underlying themes can provide insight into the specific challenges you face. Just be sure to seek feedback and alternative perspectives from people whose professional opinions you trust. Reach out to trusted colleagues or mentors who can provide an outside perspective on your abilities and achievements. They may be able to offer insights that help you recognize patterns of self-doubt or validate your accomplishments. This is because objective feedback can help counteract the distorted self-perception often associated with imposter syndrome. Moreover, the more your imposter syndrome and its underlying thoughts are proven wrong, the less likely it is to have a stronghold on you.

That being said, journaling and self-reflection should not be underestimated because they allow you to come back to your thoughts when you're in a different state of mind. You don't necessarily have to come back to your journal when you're feeling a bit more rational in your line of thinking, but your line of thinking does have to be different than what it was when you initially journaled. This will show you how your perspective can change with time and the impact of the distance between yourself and the event or thought that triggered your imposter syndrome. Engage in regular journaling or self-reflection exercises to explore your thoughts, emotions, and patterns of behavior. Write down situations or triggers that evoke feelings of self-doubt and imposter syndrome. As you continue documenting these experiences, you will gain deeper clarity on the specific type of imposter syndrome you may be experiencing. Just remember that professional help is always available for any manner of mental health issue. This, however, is something that we'll look at in upcoming chapters.

*

When you peel back the signs and symptoms of the various types of imposter syndrome, it's easy to see how they intersect and overlap. It is, nonetheless, imperative that we get to the root of our own type of imposter syndrome as a matter of urgency in unraveling what could be holding us back from our full potential.

JB

CHAPTER 4

RECOGNIZING THE SIGNS OF SELF–DOUBT AND IMPOSTER SYNDROME

In our journey to overcome self-doubt and imposter syndrome, it is essential to first recognize the signs and symptoms that manifest in our thoughts, emotions, and behaviors. This chapter delves into the importance of recognizing these signs as a crucial step toward understanding and addressing the challenges of self-doubt and imposter syndrome.

Self-doubt and imposter syndrome often lurk in the shadows, disguising themselves as normal insecurities or fleeting moments of uncertainty. However, their impact can be immense. One of the worst of all of the effects is the prevention from realizing our full potential. What's worse is that they are slow-growing phenomena, which means that they are harder to pick up on than other (more common) issues that are felt by a leader in a high-octane environment. Simply put, the frequency with which imposter syndrome symptoms are felt seems to increase with the level of intensity of stress in one's life. This is a bit of a dog chasing its own tail scenario because the more stressed you become, the more intensely you'll feel your symptoms. The more intensely you feel your symptoms, the more stressed you'll become. And so on the story goes.

Therefore, gaining awareness of the signs of self-doubt and imposter syndrome will empower you to identify and confront these challenges head-on. After all, without being consciously aware of the symptoms, they can sneak up on you and come on strong when you're in your most vulnerable (stressed) state.

Take heed that the signs of self-doubt and imposter syndrome can manifest in various ways, both internally and externally. Let's go over them again now.

> Internally, we may experience persistent feelings of inadequacy, an excessive fear of failure, or a constant need for external validation. Our thoughts may be plagued with self-criticism, negative self-talk, and a tendency to downplay our achievements. Emotionally, we may grapple with anxiety, stress, and a persistent sense of being an imposter despite evidence of our competence. These internal indicators often undermine our confidence, erode our self-esteem, and create a constant state of self-doubt.
>
> Externally, the signs of self-doubt and imposter syndrome may manifest in our behaviors and interactions. We may shy away from taking on new challenges or

> opportunities, fearing that we will be exposed as frauds. We might attribute our successes to luck or external factors, downplaying our own abilities. Procrastination, perfectionism, and excessive over-preparation are also common manifestations as we strive to avoid making mistakes or being perceived as incapable.

Now, let's look at some of the more common signs and symptoms.

Common Signs & Symptoms

Some of the more common signs and symptoms are those that we've just touched on, but it's time for us to expose these in greater detail. I cannot stress the importance of understanding one's own symptoms enough because those very symptoms can be debilitating, leading to a lack of confidence, diminished self-esteem, and a persistent fear of being exposed as a fraud. Understanding the common symptoms of self-doubt and imposter syndrome is crucial in recognizing these patterns and addressing them effectively.

So, let's start with **negative self-talk**. Individuals experiencing self-doubt and imposter syndrome often engage in negative self-talk, constantly criticizing and doubting their abilities. They may belittle their achievements and constantly compare themselves unfavorably to others. This negative self-talk reinforces feelings of inadequacy and perpetuates the cycle of self-doubt. This is why it is so important to be aware of the energy that you surround yourself with. Being surrounded by people who feed into a negative frame of mind will be incredibly detrimental to you as someone who suffers from imposter syndrome. This is because your mind is like a sponge. It will use what you feed it as ammunition to bolster your existing belief system. If your beliefs are rooted in the negativity of the imposter syndrome cycle, you are going to be using every bit of negativity or negative energy around you to stoke the fires of that mentality. Psychologists across the professional spectrum have agreed on this sentiment for decades, with several studies related to the way other people speak to us—especially people who are influential in our lives— and how we then speak to ourselves and, furthermore, go on to perform as a result. [2]

However, self-talk isn't the only manifestation of imposter syndrome that you need to start keeping a lookout for. Despite the fact that negative brain chatter has the propensity to come on quite quickly in times of stress, the issue of perfectionism (which we also explored earlier) is one of the hallmark signs. The relentless pursuit of perfection can become so forceful and loud in our lives that it stops us in our tracks. To put it plainly, we might become so inclined toward perfection that we're unable to actually get any tasks done because we believe we are incapable of attaining the level of perfection that the task requires. This is a perplexing symptom because it can happen to individuals who have completed such tasks successfully in the past and, therefore, know that they are capable of doing so again. Yet, despite this historic evidence, they stagnate and drag their feet—not because they are lazy but because their nervous system is profoundly dysregulated by the barrage of brain chatter that tells them they cannot complete what is in front of them. If you find that you're struggling to start, manage, or complete tasks that were once seemingly easy or manageable for you, you may be setting unattainable standards for yourself and attempting to have flawless scores in all aspects of life. Any deviation from perfection might be viewed as a failure, further fueling your self-doubt and anxiety.

This then feeds into the fear of failure. If you're experiencing imposter syndrome, you might have an intense fear of failure. You may avoid taking risks or pursuing challenging opportunities due to the overwhelming anxiety associated with potential failure. This fear of failure becomes a self-fulfilling prophecy, as mentioned earlier, thus preventing you from taking even a single step in the right direction, let alone fulfilling your potential. For many individuals, there are defining moments or a single defining moment in their lives that leads to this fear. If you think back to your childhood, you were practically fearless. Climbing a giant tree in your backyard or down at the park was just a passing activity that you completed without even batting an eyelid. The higher you climbed, the more fun you had! Getting as high up on a swing was a thrill, and being at the very top of a teeter-totter was giggle-inducing. Fear wasn't a word that stood out in your vocabulary. If it did, you probably wouldn't have climbed trees or learned how to ride a bike. In fact, you probably wouldn't have even learned how to walk! But somewhere along the way, you made a mistake in your life. You missed a figurative step, or things just didn't go according to plan. If you didn't have adequate support at that point in your life—and adequate support from the right places—you most likely held on to that moment as a sign of weakness on your part. You failed—or at least that's what you told yourself, along with the naysayers in your life. It could have been something as simple as dropping the ball on a specific project and not receiving the support you needed from peers, colleagues, or higher-ups. If you were, instead, chastised and lambasted for it, you might have begun to believe that your mistake was catastrophic. Despite the fact that the company in question is still thriving and you have not spontaneously combusted as you might have believed you would, you think that this is a sign that you are destined to destroy whatever you place your hands on. So, you continue working in your field because that's what you know—and yet you're never fully "in." You've got one foot out of the door in your mind because you believe that you are no longer capable of completing the tasks that you were once accustomed to breezing through.

In most cases, this is closely related to discounting your achievements. Individuals with imposter syndrome tend to downplay or dismiss their accomplishments. They attribute success to external factors such as luck, timing, or other people's support rather than acknowledging their own abilities and hard work. This undermines their confidence and reinforces feelings of being an imposter.

What worsens this is the following double-edged sword:

> **All good things = Luck or externally influenced**
>
> **All bad things = Your fault or something you could have avoided**

It's a perpetual hamster wheel of self-blame and praise for anyone and everyone other than yourself. This will, inevitably, put you in a position of overworking and overpreparing as you believe that something bad is always around the corner as the result of your perceived "incompetence." This is a common coping mechanism for those experiencing imposter syndrome. If you find yourself feeling the need to constantly prove yourself, leading to excessive hours spent on tasks and an inability to relax or enjoy your achievements, you might very well be suffering from imposter syndrome. It's almost as if you believe that if you slow down—even if it's for just a minute—you'll finally slip up and be found out for the fraud that you might think you are.

If you're not careful, all of these symptoms will boil over, and your nervous system will become so overwhelmed that you'll find yourself procrastinating over the simplest of tasks. This is because procrastination isn't actually a sign of laziness or a lack of discipline. Procrastination is often a symptom of overwhelm and an inability to get out of one's heightened stress response. This is one of the most painful paradoxes for a high-achieving individual who suffers from imposter syndrome because the fear of not meeting their own high standards or the fear of being exposed as a fraud can paralyze them, causing them to delay or avoid tasks altogether. Procrastination reinforces feelings of inadequacy and can lead to a vicious cycle of guilt and crippling self-doubt.

When these people finally complete the tasks at hand—and, in most cases, within record time—they have difficulty accepting praise. They may feel unworthy of recognition and dismiss positive feedback as insincere or undeserved. It could be because they've completed the task so quickly at the very last minute that they feel as though they didn't truly offer their best. Moreover, regardless of the fact that the task was completed to a high standard (even though it was seemingly rushed), the imposter syndrome sufferer will feel even more like a fraud because of the manner in which they completed the task in the first place. It truly is a difficult condition to grapple with.

It is important to note that not everyone will experience all of these symptoms, and the severity can vary. Additionally, the symptoms of self-doubt and imposter syndrome may fluctuate over time or be triggered by specific situations or achievements. That being said, just because you're experiencing one symptom and not any others, that doesn't mean that you're not dealing with imposter syndrome. On the opposite side of that coin, just because you're experiencing a plethora of these symptoms, that doesn't mean that you're truly dealing with imposter syndrome and not any other form of mental health condition. Social anxiety, for example, has many symptoms that are similar to imposter syndrome. If you're uncertain of the condition that you're dealing with, it's important to speak to someone who might be able to shed some light on what you're going through.

Now, let's look at the effect that these symptoms can have on you and your daily life.

The Effects of the Symptoms

The effects of the symptoms of imposter syndrome are long-reaching and can be felt throughout multiple areas of one's life. What's more, they can greatly diminish your ability to perform in all these areas of life, which can make you feel as though your feelings of being an imposter are valid.

To begin with, you might notice an uptick in your limited self-beliefs paired with diminished confidence. When plagued by self-doubt and imposter syndrome, individuals often underestimate their abilities and potential. They constantly question their skills and talents, leading to a lack of confidence in their personal and professional pursuits. This lack of self-belief can prevent individuals from taking on new challenges, pursuing opportunities, or expressing their ideas and opinions. One of the most awful results of this centers around the fact that valuable solutions to real-world problems could end up lying dormant inside the mind of the "imposter."

This then leads to issues such as missed opportunities and limited career progression. This self-imposed limitation can lead to feelings of stagnation and unfulfillment. This, in turn, will give rise to impaired decision-making and excessive self-criticism. The fear of making mistakes or being perceived as incompetent can paralyze decision-making processes. Individuals may second-guess their choices, overanalyze outcomes, or avoid making decisions altogether. This pattern of excessive self-criticism and indecision can hinder productivity, inhibit problem-solving abilities, and contribute to a cycle of frustration.

If you think it all ends there, you'd be wrong. You may struggle to accept compliments and feel undeserving of support and recognition from others. Moreover, because of the fear that others will discover your perceived inadequacies, you may isolate yourself. This can lead to feelings of loneliness, a lack of connection, and hindered collaboration or teamwork in professional settings.

At the end of the day, this will have a serious effect on your mental and emotional well-being. The persistent presence of self-doubt and imposter syndrome will negatively impact how you relate to yourself, and you may experience heightened levels of stress, leading to feelings of burnout, exhaustion, and even depression. The constant internal struggle and negative self-perception can erode self-esteem. As you struggle to let go of every single minor indiscretion or mistake from your past, everything will become amplified. You'll find yourself worrying about things that everyone else has long forgotten about and wondering whether people think less of you as a result of those mishaps. This is why addressing these detrimental effects will require you to cultivate self-awareness and develop strategies to counteract them.

By recognizing the negative consequences of these symptoms, you can prioritize your well-being, build resilience, and take steps toward embracing your abilities instead of downplaying them. For this, however, you might need to seek help.

Seeking Help

One effective way to recognize and address imposter syndrome is by speaking to people you trust, including mentors, friends, or family members. My only piece of advice in this area is to seek counsel with people whose advice you can *actually* trust. If you know for certain that the person you're speaking with has nothing to gain from either your success or your failure, that is one sign that they are the right person for the job. Equally important is gauging whether or not they have the aptitude to handle the situation you're facing. Addressing your issues through the counsel of those who aren't self-aware (or at least trying to be) on their own journey is like having a death wish for your career.

That being said, sharing your experiences and feelings with others can provide valuable insights and support, thus helping you gain perspective and validation.

For starters, gaining an external perspective will help you when you are trapped in the cycle of self-doubt and imposter syndrome. This is mainly because outsiders can see us objectively when we are unable to see ourselves in that light. Speaking with trusted individuals allows us to gain an external perspective on our achievements, skills, and abilities. They can provide an unbiased viewpoint, highlighting strengths and accomplishments that we may be overlooking or dismissing.

Their feedback can serve as a reality check—helping to dispel the negative self-perception associated with imposter syndrome.

This borders validation and reassurance quite closely. Sharing your experiences of imposter syndrome with trusted individuals can be validating. They can assure you that your feelings are not uncommon and that many high-achieving individuals experience similar doubts and fears. Their reassurance can help you realize that imposter syndrome does not reflect your true competence or worth. Moreover, if they are someone who you look up to in a professional light, hearing how they have tackled their own imposter syndrome can help you understand just how prevalent the issue is. Their validation and understanding will create a supportive environment where you can feel accepted and encouraged.

From there, gaining valuable perspectives and insights becomes that much easier. Conversations with mentors and trusted individuals will allow you to tap into their experience and wisdom. As mentioned before, they have likely encountered imposter syndrome themselves or have guided others through similar challenges. Their advice, guidance, and personal anecdotes can shed light on strategies for overcoming imposter syndrome and navigating career challenges. Their perspectives can help you reframe your thoughts, challenge negative self-beliefs, and develop a more empowered mindset.

But you have to be open to constructive feedback to truly tap into these people as resources. By sharing your experiences with them, they can provide specific feedback on areas for improvement and help you develop an action plan for personal and professional growth. This feedback, coupled with their support, can foster a sense of progression and accomplishment, thus mitigating the effects of imposter syndrome. Once you have some form of progress in motion, it will be easier to keep the momentum going.

Furthermore, having trusted advisors or mentors that you can turn to will provide you with the accountability and support that you need to navigate your leadership role. Having people who can check in on your progress, offer encouragement, and help you stay on track with your goals will prove invaluable. Their support can act as a source of motivation and inspiration during challenging times. Knowing that you have a support system that believes in you can bolster your confidence and resilience, making it easier to navigate imposter syndrome. Plus, the idea that someone else knows where you are and where you should be going can keep the embers beneath you going—fueling you into taking action even in the face of fear. Ultimately, engaging in open and honest conversations with trusted individuals and mentors can play a crucial role in recognizing and addressing imposter syndrome. Remember that you don't have to face imposter syndrome alone. Reaching out to others can be a transformative step toward growth and self-acceptance. If you're still unsure whether or not you are truly grappling with imposter syndrome, have a look at "Exercise 1: Identifying Your Imposter Syndrome" in your accompanying workbook.

*

Recognizing these signs is the first step toward reclaiming our confidence and combating self-doubt and imposter syndrome. By becoming aware of our thoughts, emotions, and behaviors, we gain insight into the underlying patterns and beliefs that contribute to our self-doubt. This awareness allows us to challenge and reframe negative thinking patterns, cultivate self-compassion, and develop strategies to overcome these challenges. By understanding and recognizing the signs of self-doubt and imposter syndrome, we can embark on a journey of self-discovery and growth. Together, let us navigate the intricacies of these challenges, unravel their impact, and equip ourselves with the tools to conquer self-doubt and imposter syndrome, paving the way for a more confident and fulfilling life.

JB

CHAPTER 5

OVERCOMING SELF–DOUBT AND IMPOSTER SYNDROME

This chapter will dive into the intricacies of overcoming self-doubt and imposter syndrome, offering insights, strategies, and inspiration to empower you on your quest for self-belief and authenticity. It explores the complex nature of these issues, highlighting the psychological and emotional factors that contribute to their development and persistence.

Both self-doubt and imposter syndrome can have far-reaching consequences in our lives. That is why it is my goal to provide individuals with the tools and insights necessary to navigate the complex terrains of self-doubt and imposter syndrome. By understanding the underlying causes and dynamics of these challenges, we can begin to dismantle their hold on our lives. Through self-reflection, self-compassion, and targeted strategies, we can develop resilience, cultivate self-belief, and reclaim our authentic voices.

In this chapter, we will explore the stories of individuals who have triumphed over self-doubt and imposter syndrome, drawing inspiration from their experiences and learning from their journeys. By examining the psychological and emotional aspects of these challenges, we can gain a deeper understanding of ourselves and the forces that shape our beliefs and perceptions.

Ultimately, overcoming self-doubt and imposter syndrome requires courage, introspection, and a commitment to growth. It is a process of self-discovery and self-empowerment that demands patience and perseverance. By exploring various strategies, exercises, and techniques, we will uncover the means to challenge negative thought patterns, reframe our self-perception, and cultivate a more confident and authentic sense of self.

Together, we will navigate the path to self-belief and unlock our true potential.

Strategies to Overcome Imposter Syndrome

Self-doubt and imposter syndrome can be debilitating, but they are not insurmountable. With the right strategies and tools, you can break free from their grip and regain your confidence. There are a variety of approaches to overcoming self-doubt and imposter syndrome, ranging from therapeutic techniques to self-reflection practices. By implementing these strategies, we can foster a positive mindset, build resilience, and reclaim our self-worth.

So, let's begin with the first item on our healing agenda: **Cognitive Behavioral Therapy (CBT)**. CBT is a widely used therapeutic approach that focuses on identifying and challenging negative thought patterns. By working with a trained therapist, you can learn to recognize distorted beliefs and replace them with more realistic and empowering thoughts. CBT helps break the cycle of self-doubt and negative self-talk, allowing you to develop a more positive and accurate perception of yourself.

If, however, you're not in a position to commit to therapy right now or you would like to try something that you can do at home right now, **mindfulness and meditation** are two practices I strongly recommend. Practicing mindfulness and meditation can help you develop a greater sense of self-awareness and detachment from negative thoughts and emotions. By observing your thoughts and emotions without judgment, you can reduce the impact of self-doubt and imposter syndrome on your mental well-being. Mindfulness practices also promote self-compassion and acceptance, allowing you to embrace your imperfections and build a healthier self-image. Finally, mindfulness practices allow you to live in the present moment, shifting your thoughts away from the brain chatter that focuses on past mistakes.

The key here is to learn the skills to be able to engage in more positive self-talk. For those of you who don't know this, your inner dialogue plays a significant role in shaping your self-perception. Positive self-talk involves consciously replacing self-critical thoughts with supportive and affirming statements. By challenging negative beliefs and reframing them in a positive light, you can cultivate a more optimistic and confident mindset. Regularly practicing positive self-talk can gradually rewire the brain, thus leading to improved self-esteem and a stronger sense of self. While it might feel like utter nonsense and a bit too farfetched for you in the beginning, it will have an impact on how you perceive yourself in the long run. This is thanks to something known as neuroplasticity, which is our "brain's ability to change, remodel and reorganize for the purpose of better ability to adapt to new situations." [3] Simply put, your brain is a pliable substance that you can mold and manipulate to your own benefit. If, however, you find that you're too far gone down the rabbit hole of imposter syndrome, but you're still reluctant to seek therapy, looking for support and guidance might be the better call.

As discussed in the previous chapter, connecting with trusted individuals, such as friends, mentors, or support groups, can provide invaluable support and guidance in overcoming self-doubt and imposter syndrome. They can help you to set realistic goals and celebrate achievements. Setting realistic goals will help you break down larger tasks into manageable steps, thus reducing the overwhelm that often accompanies self-doubt and imposter syndrome. By focusing on achievable objectives, you can build a track record of success and boost your confidence. It is equally important to celebrate your achievements, no matter how small. This will help reinforce a positive self-image and acknowledge your personal growth.

Once you have a healthy balance of small wins and past "failures," you will learn to embrace failure. More importantly, you'll start to feel grateful for the obstacles in your life as you cultivate the ability to learn from your mistakes. Failure is an inevitable part of life, and embracing it as an opportunity for growth can help overcome self-doubt. Viewing failures as valuable learning experiences rather than proof of incompetence reframes the narrative and encourages resilience. By understanding that setbacks are normal and can provide opportunities for improvement, you can approach challenges with a growth mindset and maintain your self-belief.

This, of course, becomes difficult to maintain without **practicing self-care**. Taking care of oneself physically, emotionally, and mentally is crucial in combating self-doubt and imposter syndrome. As the saying goes, you cannot pour from an empty cup. If you're not taking the time to actively and consciously refill your own cup, you're going to find yourself on the verge of burnout, which will feed into your imposter syndrome. Engaging in activities that promote relaxation, such as regular exercise, hobbies, or spending time in nature, will help to reduce stress and foster a positive mindset. However, nature walks and bubble baths aren't for everyone. Sometimes, engaging in an activity that can soothe an overstimulated nervous system or worn-out physical vessel will be just what the doctor ordered. The issue is that many of us don't know ourselves well enough to know what self-care looks like to us as unique individuals. We've gone our entire lives people-pleasing and putting ourselves last in the name of pursuing our achievements, and it can be difficult to break ourselves of these patterns and habits. Nonetheless, finding a way to prioritize self-care activities and setting boundaries will allow you to recharge and nurture your well-being, thus enabling you to approach challenges with renewed energy and confidence.

At that point, you can consider continual learning and skill development as a way to combat the idea that you are not as skilled at your job as others think you are. Just be aware that certification hoarding can manifest as one of the unhealthy means of coping with imposter syndrome. The constant need to acquire accolades is a way of placating the thought that you are not worthy of the recognition that you've received, but this can become all-consuming and take up valuable time in your life that you could dedicate elsewhere. That isn't to say that acquiring knowledge and certifications is not a worthy pursuit, but, as with all things, it needs to be done for the right reasons. That said, building competence in areas of interest can not only enhance professional growth but also boost self-confidence. Engaging in continuous learning, whether through formal education, workshops, or independent study, expands your knowledge and skills and helps to reduce your self-doubt. Acquiring new expertise can reinforce your belief in your abilities and provide evidence of your competence.

Just remember that overcoming self-doubt and imposter syndrome is an ongoing process that requires patience and persistence. By implementing these strategies, you can gradually shift your mindset, challenge your self-limiting beliefs, and cultivate a more confident and authentic sense of self. But these methods aren't foolproof. Since we were all raised in different circumstances and have been exposed to varying degrees of challenges throughout our lives, we're bound to react to these modalities differently. I don't want you to lose hope if one strategy does not work for you. There is always another method to help rid you of imposter syndrome when it seems like all else has failed.

When All Else Fails

Imposter syndrome, self-doubt, and insecurities can be particularly challenging for leaders navigating professional spaces. The pressure to prove oneself and meet societal expectations, all while faced with a dearth of transformational role models in leadership, can exacerbate these feelings. Seeking support from a therapist can provide a safe and confidential space to explore and address these concerns. Therapists are trained professionals who can guide you through a transformative journey of self-discovery and self-acceptance. Depending on the underlying issue that has brought on your imposter syndrome and the type of imposter syndrome that you're dealing with, your therapist might recommend a number of techniques or even other practitioners to help you navigate your path to mental recovery. This is the predominant reason why identifying underlying beliefs and patterns is often the first port of call.

Therapists can help leaders identify the underlying beliefs and patterns contributing to their imposter syndrome and self-doubt. Through exploration and reflection, individuals can gain insight into their thoughts, emotions, and behaviors. This, in turn, can uncover deep-seated insecurities or self-sabotaging tendencies. This understanding is crucial in dismantling negative self-perceptions and developing healthier coping mechanisms. Only then will you be able to challenge distorted thinking. Your therapist can further assist in identifying and reframing negative self-talk. They can then guide you in replacing self-critical thoughts with more balanced and realistic perspectives. It's important to note that therapeutic modalities take time, as you will need to unpack and retool several areas of your thought processes and beliefs.

The important thing is that you find the means to build self-compassion and self-acceptance. Alongside your therapist, you will cultivate a kind and nurturing relationship with yourself, fostering a sense of worthiness and self-love. This self-compassion allows leaders to acknowledge their achievements, embrace their imperfections, and treat themselves with kindness and understanding.

When you accept that there is work to be done, you can get to work on developing coping strategies that will be healthier in the long run. Working collaboratively with your therapist to develop personalized coping strategies to manage imposter syndrome and self-doubt may include stress reduction techniques, assertiveness training, and boundary-setting skills. If need be, addressing past trauma will come into play. Past experiences of discrimination, bias, or trauma can contribute to imposter syndrome and self-doubt in modern-day leaders. Therapy provides a safe space to process and heal from these experiences. Therapists use evidence-based trauma therapies to address the impact of past trauma, enabling leaders to move forward with resilience and reclaim their sense of self. If this is something you feel you have experienced in the past [4], then therapy is definitely the way to go.

Other than all of these mentioned benefits of working with a therapist, you will also find that you empower yourself in your decision-making and leadership skills. Being able to identify a problem and dive headlong into rectifying it is no easy feat—especially when it concerns the inner workings of your life and your mind. Not only this, but therapy will allow you to clarify your values, identify your strengths, and align your actions with your authentic self. In the end, you'll be able to develop a leadership style that is true to yourself.

It is important to note that therapy is a collaborative process and finding the right therapist is crucial. To begin your end of this collaborative partnership, there are a few questions that you can have the answers to before your first therapy session. These questions and answers will help your therapist understand what you're battling. To help you prepare yourself, I've cultivated a list of questions you can use pre-therapy. You will find this in your workbook as "Exercise 2: Pre-Therapy Q & A." Note that even if you don't opt for therapy, these questions will still give you insight into your thought processes.

The Proof is in the Pudding

Once you've begun working on your imposter syndrome, it's important to start looking at evidence of it among successful people. After all, imposter syndrome is a common experience that can affect individuals across various industries and leadership roles. This is good news for you because it means that many successful individuals have managed to overcome imposter syndrome and achieve remarkable success in their careers. Their stories serve as powerful examples of resilience, determination, and the ability to rise above self-doubt. One such example is

Sheryl Sandberg. As the Chief Operating Officer of Facebook and author of *Lean In*, Sheryl Sandberg has openly discussed her experiences with imposter syndrome. Despite her impressive career and accomplishments, she has acknowledged feeling like a fraud and questioning her abilities. Sandberg's willingness to share her vulnerability has inspired many, and she encourages individuals to embrace their fears and lean into their strengths.

This was something that the former **First Lady of the United States, Michelle Obama**, also prioritized in her various demanding roles. She has shared her journey of overcoming imposter syndrome. In her memoir *Becoming*, she discusses her early experiences of feeling like a fraud and not belonging. Despite her doubts, she embraced her unique voice and made significant contributions in areas such as education and health. To this day, she encourages individuals to embrace their authenticity and believe in their worth. If a former First Lady, accomplished attorney, and author can experience imposter syndrome, we all can too.

From First Ladies to CEOs, Howard Schultz is next on our list of imposter syndrome sufferers. The former Chairman and CEO of Starbucks has spoken about imposter syndrome despite his transformational impact on the coffee industry. Schultz has openly spoken on his view that few could step into a role that gargantuan and **not** feel a sense of self-doubt.

Sentiments like this aren't just shared by captains of industry but by leaders in a diverse range of fields. Take Donald Glover as a prime example. As a successful actor, rapper, director, and producer, Donald Glover should be uber-confident, right? Well, you might think so, but he has candidly discussed feeling like an imposter in various creative pursuits. This was particularly heightened when he was first hired for a creative writing position on the hit series *30 Rock*. Had he allowed his self-limiting thoughts to get in the way of his career, we wouldn't have Golden Globe-winning shows like *Atlanta,* among many others.

Sometimes, you just have to keep going and try one more time—even in the face of adversity. That was the case for celebrated chef and restaurateur Wolfgang Puck, who has admitted to grappling with imposter syndrome despite his culinary innovations and global success. Puck has been recorded by several publications as saying that he still gets a case of imposter syndrome when he's on the verge of opening a new restaurant. This is coming from a chef who has been awarded two Michelin Stars and various other awards.

These individuals demonstrate that imposter syndrome does not discriminate based on accomplishments or status. It can affect anyone, irrespective of their background, achievements, or personal beliefs. In fact, the more successful the individual, the more intense the imposter syndrome seems to be. Nevertheless, their stories also highlight the possibility of overcoming imposter syndrome and achieving greatness. The journeys of these successful individuals offer valuable lessons for those grappling with imposter syndrome. These leaders have proven that imposter syndrome does not define one's capabilities and that it is possible to reach extraordinary heights by persisting in the face of self-doubt.

As we continue on this journey, we will move on to building inner confidence. Since imposter syndrome often erodes self-confidence first, this is a crucial part of healing this condition and learning how to manage its effects. Let's explore this now.

JB

CHAPTER 6
DISMANTLING THE INNER CRITIC

Confidence is a powerful asset that empowers leaders to navigate challenges, make tough decisions, and inspire others. It is a fundamental quality for effective leadership. Developing inner confidence is a transformative journey that can positively impact one's ability to lead with conviction and authenticity. Building inner confidence involves:

- Cultivating a strong sense of self,
- Recognizing personal strengths and values,
- Embracing a growth mindset, and
- Practicing self-care and self-compassion.

It's no wonder these correlate with eradicating imposter syndrome since it centers around the erosion of self-confidence.

The question is, how can we go about building inner confidence?

Building inner confidence begins with developing a deep understanding and acceptance of oneself. It requires the exploration of personal beliefs, values, and aspirations to create a solid foundation of self-awareness. When leaders have clarity about who they are and what they stand for, they can authentically communicate their vision. Additionally, they can inspire trust and effectively lead others.

Recognizing and leveraging personal strengths is another crucial aspect of building inner confidence. Each individual possesses unique talents, skills, and qualities that contribute to their leadership potential. By identifying and embracing these strengths, leaders can tap into their full potential and build confidence in their abilities. Additionally, understanding personal values and aligning them with leadership practices helps leaders stay grounded. It helps them to make principled decisions and earn the respect and trust of their teams.

A growth mindset is invaluable for building inner confidence. Embracing a growth mindset means believing in the potential for personal and professional growth and development. Leaders with a growth mindset view challenges and setbacks as stepping stones toward success. They are willing to take risks, learn from failures, and continuously adapt or grow. Cultivating a growth mindset allows leaders to overcome self-doubt and embrace new challenges with confidence and resilience.

Self-care and self-compassion play a vital role in building inner confidence. Taking care of oneself physically, mentally, and emotionally is essential for maintaining well-being and fostering a positive mindset. Prioritizing self-care activities such as exercise, adequate rest, and engaging in activities that bring joy and relaxation allows leaders to recharge and maintain their energy levels. Similarly, self-compassion involves treating oneself with kindness and understanding. It's important to embrace one's imperfections and practice positive self-talk. By practicing self-care and self-compassion, leaders can boost their self-esteem, reduce self-doubt, and foster a strong sense of inner confidence.

Now that you know all of this, keep in mind that building inner confidence is an ongoing process that requires self-reflection, dedication, and a willingness to step outside of your comfort zone. It involves embracing personal growth, embracing strengths and values, and developing a positive mindset. When you cultivate inner confidence, you'll not only elevate your own leadership abilities but also inspire and empower those around you. It becomes a ripple effect, creating a culture of confidence, collaboration, and success within your respective organization.

Through the transformative practices that you're about to learn in this chapter, you can unlock your full potential. If you're ready to lead with authenticity and conviction—and make a positive impact in their personal and professional lives—let's dive in.

Looking Toward Limiting Self-Beliefs

Limiting beliefs and self-doubt are internal obstacles that hold us back, restrict our potential, and prevent us from achieving our goals. However, by recognizing and challenging these limiting beliefs, we can break free from their grip and begin cultivating a mindset of self-belief and empowerment. While limiting beliefs have been touched on several times as a broad concept, I haven't picked it apart and explained it thoroughly, which is precisely what I'll be doing now.

Limiting beliefs are deeply ingrained thoughts or assumptions that constrain our thinking and actions. They are often rooted in past experiences, societal conditioning, or negative self-perception. These beliefs create a self-imposed limitation on what we believe we can achieve or become. Common examples include thoughts like **"I'm not good enough," "I don't deserve success,"** or **"I'll never be able to do that."** These beliefs are often unfounded and can severely hinder our progress.

The first step in overcoming limiting beliefs is to recognize and identify them. Take time to reflect on your thoughts and patterns of self-talk. Pay attention to the recurring negative beliefs that arise in different areas of your life. Once identified, challenge these beliefs by seeking evidence to the contrary. Actively look for instances where you have succeeded, received positive feedback, or accomplished something you previously believed was beyond your capabilities. For instance, when you tell yourself that you're not strong enough to lead your team, try to think back to times when you exhibited the type of strength that you believe is required of your leadership role.

Another effective strategy is to reframe your limiting beliefs into empowering statements. Instead of saying, **"I'm not good enough,"** reframe it as **"I am capable of learning and growing."** By shifting your perspective, you create space for growth and self-improvement. Practicing affirmations and positive self-talk to reinforce these new empowering beliefs is essential. For affirmations that you can use or tweak, be sure to turn to "Exercise 3: Using Positive Affirmations" in your workbook now.

These affirmations need to be strong and relevant because self-doubt often accompanies limiting beliefs and can undermine our confidence and decision-making abilities. It arises from a lack of trust in our skills, knowledge, or worthiness. Overcoming self-doubt requires a combination of self-reflection, self-compassion, and action. One approach to overcoming self-doubt is to challenge the validity of your doubts by gathering evidence of your capabilities, as mentioned before. To do this, make a list of you're accomplishments as well as the skills and strengths you believe you used to accomplish them. Reflect on past successes and moments where you demonstrated competence or received positive feedback. These reminders can help counteract the negative self-talk and reinforce your belief in your abilities.

It's important to begin engaging in activities that bring you joy and a sense of accomplishment. Set realistic goals that are manageable and actually achievable. Then, make sure to celebrate your achievements along the way. Surround yourself with supportive and encouraging individuals who believe in your abilities. Do whatever it takes to get back in touch with your most authentic self—the person beneath all the expectations and doubts wrongfully thrust upon them. Practicing this level of self-compassion is vital when dealing with self-doubt. Treat yourself with kindness and understanding, recognizing that everyone experiences doubts and setbacks.

Bear in mind that it's not all about thought processes and the energy you surround yourself with. Taking action is key to breaking free from self-doubt. Often, we wait for our confidence to magically appear before taking steps toward our goals. However, confidence is built through action and experience. Start with small, manageable steps and gradually increase the difficulty. Each step forward will reinforce your belief in yourself and contribute to your overall growth and self-confidence.

It's important to remember that overcoming limiting beliefs and self-doubt is an ongoing process. It requires consistent effort and self-awareness. Be patient with yourself. This is all a part of the journey anyway. With a solid sense of self-compassion and a good support system in place, you will find it that much easier to develop a growth mindset.

Developing a Growth Mindset

A growth mindset is one that doesn't accept the idea that talent is inherent. Instead, it is rooted in the belief that our abilities, as well as our intelligence, can be enhanced through our own efforts. It is a powerful tool for overcoming self-doubt and imposter syndrome as it enables us to embrace challenges, persist in the face of setbacks, and see failures as opportunities for growth. By cultivating a growth mindset, we can transform our self-talk from negative and self-defeating to positive and empowering.

To develop a growth mindset, it is essential to shift your perspective on failure. Instead of viewing failure as a reflection of your worth or competence, you should see it as a stepping stone toward improvement and learning. Embrace challenges as opportunities to stretch beyond your comfort zone and acquire new skills. Understand that setbacks are a natural part of the learning process and that with perseverance and effort, you can overcome them. To begin seeing things this way, you need to be able to look at your past mistakes and supposed failures through a somewhat objective lens. Doing your best to find the lesson in the past distress will give you the clarity you need to eradicate your fixed mindset.

Positive self-talk plays a crucial role in reinforcing a growth mindset. It involves replacing negative thoughts and self-criticism with supportive and empowering statements. Pay attention to your internal dialogue and challenge any self-limiting beliefs or self-defeating thoughts that arise. Again, reframing can assist you in this regard. Instead of saying, **"I can't do this,"** replace it with **"I may not be able to do it yet, but with effort and practice, I can."** By reframing negative self-talk, you can cultivate a more optimistic and resilient mindset.

Moving on.

One effective strategy for incorporating positive self-talk into your daily life is to use affirmations. You can create your own affirmations based on your unique circumstances and then repeat these affirmations regularly—both verbally and in writing. For example, you might say, **"I am capable of overcoming challenges"** or **"I am worthy of success and recognition."** You can rewire your thought patterns and strengthen your self-confidence by consistently reinforcing these positive beliefs.

Another helpful technique for reinforcing these positive beliefs is to visualize success and imagine yourself achieving your goals. Create a mental image of yourself performing at your best, overcoming obstacles, and experiencing the satisfaction of accomplishing your objectives. Visualization can help program your mind for success and increase your belief in your abilities. This is because your brain can't actually tell the difference between reality and your imagination. All thoughts—both those that you create when interacting with the world around you and those created with your imagination—are processed in the same way. Therefore, what you think, your mind will accept as reality, and this will empower you. Also, when you frame your success as something inevitable and see what it might look like in your mind's eye, you make it a possibility that your mind will work toward.

Mindfulness practices can also aid in developing a growth mindset and positive self-talk. To become more mindful, you will need to learn to be present in the moment—becoming nonjudgmental of your feelings and thoughts about yourself. By cultivating mindfulness, you can gain awareness of negative thought patterns and consciously choose to reframe them into more positive and supportive thoughts. Engaging in meditation, deep breathing exercises, or journaling can help foster mindfulness and self-awareness. You can also opt for mindfulness in the moment, which can entail:

- Watching a drop of water glide across your shower surface in the morning,

- Taking small and conscious bites while you're eating, or

- Becoming mindful of the sensations in your body at any given moment.

It's important to note that developing a growth mindset and using positive self-talk takes time and practice. Don't be too hard on yourself if you're unable to develop the level of mindfulness you would like to within a matter of weeks. Be patient with yourself as you navigate this newfound way of engaging with your inner mind. Surround yourself with positive influences and seek support from mentors, coaches, or like-minded individuals who can provide guidance and encouragement. By cultivating a growth mindset and using positive self-talk, you can transform your inner dialogue and boost your self-confidence. Add to this to your newfound ability to leverage personal strengths and values, and you'll be practically unstoppable on your path to winning the war against imposter syndrome.

Leveraging Personal Strengths & Values

This is a strategy that works like a charm. By recognizing your unique talents and aligning your actions with your core values, you can build self-confidence and overcome the persistent feelings of being an imposter.

To begin, take the time to reflect on your personal strengths. These are the qualities and skills that come naturally to you and make you stand out. Consider your achievements, both big and small, and identify the strengths that contributed to your success. These strengths can include attributes like problem-solving abilities, creativity, leadership skills, adaptability, or empathy. Acknowledging and accepting these strengths is an important step in combating imposter syndrome.

Next, align your actions and choices with your core values. Core values are the fundamental principles that guide your behavior and shape your sense of purpose. They reflect what truly matters to you in life and work. Take the time to clarify your values and ensure that your actions are in line with them. When your actions align with your values, you experience a greater sense of authenticity and confidence, which can counter the feelings of being an imposter.

Leveraging your strengths and values involves intentionally applying them in your personal and professional endeavors. This means intentionally utilizing your strengths to tackle challenges and make meaningful contributions. It also means making decisions that align with your values, even when faced with pressure or external expectations. By focusing on your strengths and values, you can build a sense of authenticity and self-assurance, gradually diminishing the effects of imposter syndrome.

It can be helpful to create a list or visual representation of your strengths and values. Write down your key strengths and the values that are most important to you. Place this list somewhere visible, such as on your desk or as a screensaver. This way, it will serve as a constant reminder of your unique qualities and guiding principles. Whenever you start doubting yourself, refer to this list to reaffirm your worth and potential.

In addition to self-reflection, seeking feedback from trusted individuals can also help in identifying and validating your strengths. Since you already know the importance and benefits of seeking counsel with trusted individuals, I'll leave this here.

Now, we can look at practicing self-care with more scrutiny.

Practicing Self-Care

Practicing self-care has—and will continue to—come up throughout this book. This is because when your sense of self-worth and confidence is diminished, self-care tends to go out the window. You'll find yourself toiling away at the office and neglecting the most basic of principles in this area of your life. As a leader, it is crucial to prioritize self-care and self-compassion to eliminate self-doubt and foster a positive mindset.

Self-care can involve engaging in activities that promote physical, mental, and emotional well-being. It encompasses practices such as maintaining a balanced lifestyle, setting boundaries, and engaging in activities that recharge and rejuvenate you. Taking care of yourself enables you to show up as your best self. It also equips you with the ability to maintain energy levels and handle challenges more effectively.

One essential aspect of self-care is prioritizing physical well-being. Regular exercise, adequate sleep, and a nutritious diet are fundamental in promoting overall health and providing the energy and mental clarity needed to navigate the demands of leadership. Sleep is especially important in this regard because many of us are not getting adequate sleep, nor are we practicing good sleep hygiene.

Good sleep hygiene includes sleeping in a cool room, making sure that there are no disturbing light sources filtering into your bedroom, and ensuring that your sleeping space is neat and free of clutter. These are among many other habits that form good sleep hygiene. If you would like to make sure that you're practicing good sleep hygiene, ensure that you tick all the boxes in "Exercise 4: Good Sleep Hygiene." As you might have already guessed, this can be found in your accompanying workbook.

After a good sleep routine, making time for hobbies, relaxation, and activities that bring joy is also crucial for recharging and reducing stress.

Engaging in activities that promote self-reflection, such as journaling, can help you gain insight into your thoughts and emotions, thus being able to address underlying self-doubt and develop resilience. Furthermore, setting realistic expectations and practicing self-acceptance will release you from the grips of overachieving. Recognize that perfection is unattainable. By prioritizing self-care and self-compassion, you can create a solid foundation for personal and professional growth. When you take care of yourself, you not only benefit your own well-being but also set an example for others.

*

When all is said and done, dismantling the inner critic requires a conscious and concerted effort. Without making an intentional decision to find the means to build your self-confidence, you will find yourself in unhealthy patterns and routines that further exacerbate the effects of imposter syndrome. As you begin whittling away at imposter syndrome, you can fill the space it once took with more positive actions, such as developing a great leadership style.

JB

CHAPTER 7

LEADERSHIP STYLES AND TRAITS FOR MODERN LEADERS

In today's rapidly evolving world, understanding and embracing the leadership styles and traits of successful leaders can pave the way for increased diversity, inclusion, and innovation in organizations as well as society as a whole.

Throughout this chapter, we will explore the distinct characteristics that modern-day leaders often embody in their approach to leadership. We will delve into the specific leadership styles and traits that have proven effective for transformational leaders, focusing on their impact, benefits, and applicability in different contexts.

One key aspect of modern leadership styles is the emphasis on collaboration and inclusivity. Successful leaders often prioritize building strong relationships, fostering teamwork, and valuing diverse perspectives. They create environments that encourage active participation, empower individuals, and promote collective decision-making. Such collaborative leadership styles can yield higher employee engagement, enhanced creativity, and better problem-solving.

Another prominent trait observed in transformational leaders is their ability to inspire and motivate others through transformational leadership. They possess a deep sense of empathy, connecting with others on an emotional level and nurturing their growth and development. This leadership style helps create a positive work culture where individuals feel supported, motivated, and empowered to reach their full potential. These leaders often exhibit a heightened level of emotional intelligence, which involves perceiving and managing emotions in oneself and others. This emotional intelligence allows them to navigate complex interpersonal dynamics, empathize with team members, and cultivate strong relationships based on trust and understanding.

This ties closely to the great significance of authenticity and vulnerability in leadership. Successful leaders are unafraid to show their true selves—embracing their strengths, weaknesses, and personal experiences. By being authentic and vulnerable, they create an environment where others feel safe to do the same, fostering a culture of openness, collaboration, and innovation.

Now, let's unpack effective leadership styles.

Effective Leadership Styles

While there is no one-size-fits-all approach, certain leadership styles and traits have proven to be particularly effective for the modern-day leader.

One leadership style that we previously touched on is transformational leadership. Transformational leaders inspire and motivate their teams by setting a compelling vision, fostering open communication, and empowering others to reach their full potential. They are adept at building relationships, nurturing talent, and creating a positive and collaborative work environment. Transformational leadership allows leaders to engage and connect with their teams, promoting a sense of shared purpose and driving exceptional results. To develop this leadership style, it's important to address your emotional intelligence (EQ). The more self-aware you become, the more heightened your EQ level will become. This, in turn, will prime you to become a transformational leader.

Another effective leadership style is democratic leadership. This style emphasizes collaboration, participation, and inclusivity in decision-making processes. By involving team members in the decision-making process, democratic leaders create a sense of ownership and commitment. Leaders who adopt a democratic leadership style foster a culture of empowerment where diverse perspectives are valued and collective wisdom is leveraged to drive innovation and problem-solving. Practicing this style of leadership, however, is easier said than done—especially if imposter syndrome is still an issue. Relinquishing control means that there is the potential of failure and a fear of failure is one of the core issues that those with imposter syndrome are faced with. If you can get past your fear of failure, this is definitely a leadership style that would be worth your while.

Then, we have the servant leadership style. Servant leaders see the needs of their team as a top priority. Furthermore, they work toward the growth of each team member. They lead by example—actively listening and empathizing with others. By focusing on the well-being and success of their team, servant leaders build trust, loyalty, and high levels of engagement. This style allows leaders to foster strong relationships, promote a sense of belonging, and create a supportive as well as nurturing work environment.

However, it doesn't just end with the styles mentioned above. There are several others that you could consider. That being said, these are the most prevalent styles that seem to work the best for modern-day leaders.

What would you consider to be your true leadership style?

If you're still uncertain, have a look at "Exercise 5: Identifying Your Leadership Style" in your workbook.

Note that it's entirely possible to blend several leadership styles to guide your team. Some moments may require a more authoritarian approach than others. Equally, some moments may call for a laissez-faire approach. Getting to know both yourself and your team so that you can establish when it's the right time for certain leadership characteristics is paramount. In addition to leadership styles, certain traits contribute to the success of leaders. As mentioned, emotional intelligence is a critical trait that enables leaders to understand and manage their emotions to effectively navigate relationships. Leaders who bring high levels of emotional intelligence to their roles prime themselves with the ability to build strong connections, resolve conflicts, and create a positive work culture.

Resilience is another important trait for leaders. The ability to bounce back from setbacks, adapt to change, and maintain a positive outlook is essential in today's dynamic and challenging business environment. Those who demonstrate resilience inspire their teams to persevere, overcome obstacles, and achieve their goals. This will undoubtedly come in handy during the seasons when things don't go according to plan. Arming yourself with a tendency toward resilience as well as effective communication skills will make you an indomitable force in your organization. This is because clear and persuasive communication allows leaders to articulate their vision, engage their teams, and build strong relationships with stakeholders. If you take the time to truly excel in communication, you will be able to inspire, influence, and motivate others toward shared objectives.

While these leadership styles and traits are often associated with successful leaders, it is important to recognize that individuals can blend different styles and traits to suit their own strengths and organizational contexts. What matters most is authenticity, self-awareness, and a commitment to continuous growth and development.

Modeling Those Who Have Gone Before Us

There are numerous examples of successful leaders who embody the traits and styles discussed—demonstrating the impact of their leadership in various fields. These leaders have broken barriers, achieved remarkable success, and inspired others through their exceptional leadership qualities. These are leaders such as Indra Nooyi, the former CEO of PepsiCo. Indra Nooyi exemplifies transformational leadership. She led the company with a clear vision and a commitment to sustainability and diversity. Nooyi fostered an inclusive culture, encouraging collaboration and innovation within the organization. This is a key sign that Nooyi chose to marry several leadership styles for the benefit of her team.

This is quite similar to Angela Merkel. As the former Chancellor of Germany, Merkel demonstrated true democratic leadership during her tenure. She valued diverse perspectives, sought consensus, and encouraged open dialogue. Merkel's leadership style emphasized inclusivity and stability, leading to her long and impactful tenure as a world leader. She is revered as a woman who was tough when she needed to be and empathic when the time called for it.

Perhaps on the slightly gentler scale is Mary Barra, the CEO of General Motors, who exemplifies both transformational and servant leadership. She successfully led the company through a period of change and transformation, focusing on innovation and the development of electric and autonomous vehicles. Barra is known for her commitment to her employees' well-being and development, creating a culture of trust and empowerment.

Equally charismatic is none other than Justin Trudeau, the Prime Minister of Canada. He represents a modern example of transformational leadership in politics. His leadership style has had a significant impact on Canada and the world stage. First, Trudeau is known for his progressive vision and commitment to diversity and inclusivity. Second, Trudeau possesses exceptional communication skills. He engages with the public through various platforms, addressing issues that matter to Canadians and emphasizing the importance of unity and diversity. His ability to connect with people of all backgrounds has contributed to a sense of national unity and pride.

Through their leadership, these people have not only achieved personal success but have also inspired others and paved the way for future generations of leaders. Take stock of what they and others just like them have overcome. Likewise, take stock of what you have overcome in your life whenever you begin to doubt whether you truly are the leader that you're meant to be. When you do this, that sneaking suspicion that you're an imposter will become less covert, and you will become more adept at mitigating its effects.

Remaining compassionate in your leadership approach—no matter which style you adopt—must always be paramount. Of course, the obstacles that come our way will always change us to some degree. That is the purpose of the fluidity and evolutionary nature of life. However, they should not shatter and rearrange the core of who we are. It's important to nurture oneself and one's strengths to truly tap into these traits. By embracing relationship building, mentorship, authenticity, and vulnerability, leaders contribute to a style that promotes inclusivity, trust, and collaboration in the workplace.

*

As we move on from this chapter, remember that countless leaders have felt precisely what you're feeling at this very moment. They have questioned their abilities—and possibly, their sanity—as they stood at the helm of projects, causes, and organizations that have gone on to shape the world. They say that hindsight is 20/20, and this is truly the case for many leaders—for it is only in looking back that they're able to see how great they've always been. In the next chapter, we'll focus on bringing that greatness into vision in the present moment, starting with your communication skills.

JB

CHAPTER 8
COMMUNICATION SKILLS FOR LEADERS

Effective communication is a cornerstone of successful leadership. In today's dynamic and diverse professional landscape, leaders must navigate various challenges and leverage their communication skills to inspire, influence, and drive positive change. Moreover, the ability to effectively communicate has become essential for establishing credibility, building relationships, and achieving organizational goals. People often fail to see the importance of effective communication and have little understanding of what it truly entails. While news outlets, the media, and various pop culture avenues have flogged the topic of effective communication for everything that it's worth, all of that buzz still doesn't provide an accurate depiction of effective communication. In fact, it is actually contrarian to the agenda of raising awareness of effective communication.

The buck stops here. In this chapter, we'll delve into the communication skills that empower leaders to articulate their vision, motivate their teams, and foster collaboration. These skills enable leaders to navigate complex situations, handle difficult conversations, and create inclusive as well as engaging work environments. As we progress, we'll highlight the importance of active listening, assertiveness, and clarity in conveying ideas and messages. Additionally, we'll explore the different learning and communication styles, thus emphasizing the need for adaptability to connect with diverse audiences.

This means that whether you are a seasoned executive, an aspiring leader, or someone seeking to improve your communication skills, this chapter will equip you with practical tools and techniques to communicate with confidence and impact. By honing your communication skills, you can effectively navigate challenges, build strong relationships, and lead with authenticity.

Why Communication is Key

Honing strong communication skills is particularly important for leaders as they navigate their roles in diverse and sometimes challenging environments. Effective communication enables leaders to convey ideas, build relationships, inspire and motivate others, and drive organizational success.

By developing excellent communication skills, leaders can effectively assert their expertise, articulate their thoughts, and assertively communicate their ideas or decisions. This is especially important for anyone entering a new organization. Clear and persuasive communication helps counter resistance and ensures that their voices are heard and respected. Now, it should go without saying, but there are certain people who will be wholly dedicated to misunderstanding you no matter how hard you try to communicate with them. Try to steer clear of the negativity bias when this happens. If you don't, you'll have one person convincing you that your communication skills—both receiving and emitting—are worthless. This will be in spite of the fact that there is more than sufficient evidence to the contrary.

Nonetheless, fostering effective communication skills will give you the confidence that you're being misunderstood because of failure on the other party's part and by no fault of your own.

If not for placing the responsibility of the negativity of others squarely on their shoulders, communication skills also create spaces where everyone feels comfortable sharing their ideas and opinions. By actively listening to others, leaders can gain insights and build real trust, which is exceptionally hard these days. This is because people tend to be guarded, especially in the workplace. They're so used to the narrative that organizations want nothing but to bleed them dry of their time and skills that many of them have given up on the idea that any form of trust can be built with a "superior" in a work environment.

However, the more a leader practices open communication, the more that others will be enabled to do the same. This will lead to informed decisions and the ability for a leader to harness the collective intelligence of their teams. This, of course, is a key driver of innovation.

Ultimately, strong communication skills allow leaders to inspire and motivate their teams. By effectively conveying their vision, values, and goals, they can rally their team members around a common purpose and create a shared sense of direction. Through their words and actions, they can inspire enthusiasm, commitment, and a sense of ownership among their team members. Excellent communication skills also help leaders to provide constructive feedback and offer recognition, something which many people find difficult to accomplish. For the most part, modern-day leaders tend to be more agreeable than traditional ones. [5] While this narrative isn't true for everyone, it is the general consensus. This, therefore, makes it hard for many leaders to give critical feedback without feeling awful in the process or going the complete opposite direction by offering the feedback in a blunt manner. Again, this is not true for everyone. But if practicing good communication has the power to ease the pressure that some leaders feel when communicating feedback, this will only work to everyone's benefit. As more professionals become aware of where they could improve and where they're going right, they'll become more astute in their roles. This, in turn, bolsters the success of the organization in question and the leader.

Having the ability to navigate complex interpersonal dynamics and build strong relationships allows leaders to truly connect with their team members on a personal level because this is how they're able to demonstrate empathy. You see, when you understand your team's needs and aspirations—and exhibit this understanding through effective communication—you build a strong level of trust. By actively communicating and demonstrating respect, you can build a rapport, which is essential for collaboration and loyalty in high-performance teams.

Finally, communication skills are vital for representing and advocating for yourself and others. You need to effectively communicate your achievements, goals, and aspirations to advance your career and overcome any self-doubt or imposter syndrome you may experience. However, you are also responsible for advocating for your team members—ensuring that their contributions are recognized and voices are heard. This is how you navigate negotiation, assert your worth, and champion diversity in your organization no matter what industry you're in.

It's clear that tackling communication will lead to more effective leadership. The next question is how do we begin to improve these communication skills?

How to Begin Improving Communication Skills

Improving communication skills is a continuous process that involves the use of practical tools and techniques. Two key tools that can significantly enhance communication skills are active listening and assertiveness training. These tools empower individuals, including leaders, to effectively convey their messages, build rapport, and navigate complex interactions.

Active listening is a basic yet crucial skill for effective communication. It involves fully engaging with the speaker—not just hearing their words but also understanding their emotions, perspectives, and underlying messages. Active listening requires focused attention, empathy, and an open mind. By practicing active listening, leaders can create an environment where team members feel heard, valued, and understood. This skill will allow you to gather valuable insights, build trust, and establish strong relationships with your team members.

To engage in active listening, you can employ several techniques. First, you can maintain eye contact and adopt an open body posture to signal your attentiveness and interest. Second, you can paraphrase and summarize what the speaker has said to you to ensure comprehension and demonstrate your understanding. Third, you can ask thoughtful and probing questions to delve deeper into the speaker's thoughts and emotions. Finally, you can provide nonverbal cues, such as nodding and using appropriate facial expressions, to indicate your engagement and encouragement.

Assertiveness training is another practical tool that helps individuals communicate their thoughts, needs, and boundaries effectively. It enables leaders to express their opinions, assert their rights, and negotiate assertively in various professional situations. Assertiveness training equips leaders with the skills to communicate confidently and respectfully, even in challenging circumstances. This is a great way to combat the feeling of needing to be agreeable at all times.

Assertiveness training involves learning and practicing specific techniques. For example, you can learn to use "I" statements to express your thoughts and feelings without blaming or accusing others. For instance, **"I feel that the Bradley Merger could have been handled better"** instead of **"You really dropped the ball with a big client."** You can also practice using assertive body language, such as maintaining an upright posture and speaking clearly and confidently. Furthermore, leaders can develop skills in setting boundaries by saying "no" when necessary and handling conflicts constructively.

To explore this in further detail and put it into practice, head over to your accompanying workbook and take a shot at "Exercise 6: Language Matters."

By incorporating these practical tools into your communication repertoire, you will enhance your effectiveness in various professional contexts. Active listening will allow you to understand and respond empathetically to the needs of your team members, thus fostering a culture of collaboration and psychological safety.

Ultimately, assertiveness training enables leaders to express their ideas and needs with confidence and clarity, thus promoting their influence and ensuring their voices are heard. It is important for leaders to engage in continuous practice and self-reflection to strengthen their communication skills. They can seek feedback, attend workshops, or participate in communication-focused training programs.

Now, let's dive deeper into the various listening and learning styles.

Understanding Listening & Communicating Styles

Active listening is, essentially, a means of learning. In this instance, it's a means of learning more about the person that you're communicating with or the circumstances at play. Understanding different learning and listening styles is essential for effective communication and information processing. People have diverse preferences when it comes to receiving and assimilating information. Recognizing these styles can greatly enhance communication and learning experiences. If you're trying to impart information, understanding how someone else learns is important. If you're trying to understand more about a person or situation, getting to know your own learning preference is crucial. Some common learning and listening styles include kinesthetic, visual, auditory, and read/write. Let's explore them now.

Kinesthetic learners prefer a hands-on, experiential approach to learning. They thrive when they can engage in physical activities, manipulate objects, and directly experience concepts. For these learners, listening is often complemented by doing. They may benefit from role-playing exercises, interactive simulations, or practical demonstrations. Kinesthetic learners tend to retain information best when they can engage multiple senses and incorporate movement into their learning experiences. Team-building activities are great opportunities for this person to learn.

Visual learners rely on visual cues and images to process information effectively. They learn best when information is presented in the form of diagrams, charts, graphs, or videos. Visual learners often take detailed notes and benefit from color coding, mind maps, or visual aids that enhance the organization and presentation of information. They excel in environments where visual materials and visual representations of concepts are provided. Presentations work exceptionally well for them.

Auditory learners prefer to process information through sound and verbal communication. They learn best when information is presented orally or through lectures, discussions, or audio recordings. These learners have a strong ability to remember and recall information through listening and discussing concepts with others. They benefit from participating in group discussions, engaging in debates, and listening to podcasts or audiobooks to enhance their understanding. This person will be fairly easy to communicate with as imparting information can be as simple as having a conversation with them.

Read/write learners have a preference for written information. They excel in reading and writing activities, such as reading textbooks, taking extensive notes, and creating written summaries or outlines. These learners often prefer to access information through written materials, such as articles, textbooks, or written instructions. They tend to organize their thoughts through writing and benefit from creating written study guides or engaging in reflective writing exercises. Creating opportunities for summary writing or report writing will help them gain insight into their own shortcomings and strong points.

It's important to note that individuals may have a combination of these learning and listening styles, with one or two styles being more dominant. Furthermore, learning styles can evolve and change over time—influenced by personal preferences and experiences. Understanding and catering to different learning and listening styles can significantly enhance communication and learning experiences. Effective communicators often employ a variety of approaches to accommodate different styles, creating a more inclusive and engaging learning environment.

By recognizing and adapting to different learning and listening styles, you can enhance your own learning experiences and improve your ability to communicate effectively with others. Furthermore, if you embrace a variety of learning and listening styles, you will afford yourself the opportunity to engage and succeed based on your unique preferences and strengths.

Once we can change the mindset that everyone learns, listens, and communicates in the same manner, we'll be able to move past frustrations and focus on solutions.

Learning From Notable Communicators

There are numerous examples of successful people who have developed strong communication skills, which have played a crucial role in their achievements and leadership positions. These people have demonstrated the power of effective communication in various fields, thus inspiring and influencing others through their words and actions.

Probably the most notable communicator of them all is someone who built an entire career out of active listening and empathy—Oprah Winfrey. As a media mogul, Oprah Winfrey has definitely built her empire on her exceptional communication skills. She possesses a unique ability to connect with her audience and create a safe as well as empathetic space for open dialogue. Winfrey's talk show served as a platform for discussing important social issues and showcasing the power of effective communication to inspire change. As one of the most beloved thought leaders in the world, her ability to provide honest feedback in tough situations without raising her voice, losing her composure, or making the other party feel in any way inferior is beyond inspirational.

We also have Simon Sinek, who is known for his powerful and relatable storytelling. He has a knack for using real-life examples and anecdotes to convey his ideas. His most famous concept, "Start with Why," encourages individuals and organizations to find their deeper purpose and communicate it effectively. Through stories and practical examples, he illustrates the transformative impact of understanding and communicating one's "why."

There is another notable leader who has taken a communicative approach where important causes are concerned. Melinda Gates, co-founder of the Bill & Melinda Gates Foundation, is renowned for her ability to communicate complex global issues in a relatable and accessible manner. Her strong communication skills have enabled her to drive meaningful conversations around topics like global health, women's empowerment, and education. Gates' clarity and passion inspire others to take action and make a difference.

These industry leaders have not only honed their communication skills but have also used them strategically to positively impact their respective fields. Through their authenticity, empathy, and ability to convey their messages effectively, they have inspired and influenced countless individuals. In turn, they have paved the way for change and progress. These examples serve as a reminder of the importance of effective communication for leaders. By developing strong communication skills, you can amplify your voice, build connections, and lead with influence.

*

If your goal is to consistently apply these practical tools and techniques, look into the communication styles of the leaders that inspire you. You can cultivate strong communication skills that enable you to effectively convey your messages, build relationships, and lead with confidence. Essentially, immerse yourself in the techniques of people who inspire you and tweak their modalities to suit you, your personality traits, and your preferences. Doing this will give you a tailored approach to communication that not only feels authentic but also comes as naturally to you as possible. In fact, with time, it will become second nature.

JB

CHAPTER 9

NAVIGATING BIAS AND DISCRIMINATION

In today's professional landscape, navigating bias and discrimination is an unfortunate reality that many leaders face. Navigating these challenges requires a thoughtful approach and a strong understanding of the dynamics at play. This chapter explores the topic of navigating bias and discrimination as a leader, highlighting the unique obstacles and complexities that you may encounter on your professional journey.

Let's look at an example regarding female leaders in particular for a minute. The fact is, there are definite biases and disparities that women still face. Female leaders often confront biases rooted in stereotypes and societal expectations, which can manifest in various ways, such as limited access to leadership roles, unequal compensation, or being overlooked for promotions. Discrimination can also intersect with other aspects of identity, such as race, ethnicity, age, or sexual orientation, further exacerbating the challenges faced by women in leadership positions.

The goal of this chapter is to shed light on the realities of bias and discrimination that leaders face, providing insights and perspectives to help them navigate these obstacles successfully. By recognizing and understanding the various forms of bias and discrimination, leaders can develop strategies to overcome these barriers and thrive in their professional lives. Moreover, it helps to know that these biases truly exist because—let's be honest—there are people who will try to gaslight you into thinking that you're not seeing (or experiencing) what you clearly are.

That said, while it is important to acknowledge the existence of bias and discrimination, it is equally crucial to focus on proactive solutions. Seeing something without actually doing something is as useful as a fork when all you've got is soup. I'm not insinuating that speaking up about discrimination isn't hard—because it is. However, the goal here is to empower leaders to navigate these challenges effectively. By examining real-world experiences and sharing practical advice, this chapter aims to equip you with the knowledge and tools necessary to confront bias, overcome obstacles, and foster an environment of inclusivity and equity.

Why?

Well, because it's as I said—it's not easy to do when you're going it alone.

Before we delve into our first subsection, it is essential to emphasize that the responsibility for addressing bias and discrimination lies not solely with the people affected but also with organizations and society at large. By raising awareness, promoting diversity and inclusion initiatives, and holding individuals and institutions accountable, we can work toward creating a more equitable and supportive environment for everyone in leadership roles.

That's really key here.

If we're going to navigate these complex dynamics, challenge stereotypes, and break down barriers, that little keyword—accountability—is going to have to be paramount. It is my sincerest hope that by shedding light on some of the more common (and uncommon) biases, leaders can be equipped with the confidence and resilience needed to thrive in the face of discrimination. If they can go on to advocate for a more inclusive and equitable future, that will be the cherry on top of the cake.

Now, let's sink our teeth into the first topic for discussion—one that has to be pinned as the undertone for all that is to follow in this chapter: it is **not** all in your head!

It's (NOT) All in Your Head

Despite the progress that we've made as a society in terms of gender equality, women continue to encounter various forms of bias and discriminatory practices that can hinder their professional growth and success. The sad reality is that we don't know until we know. You can hear about these things happening to other women—maybe even women that you know on somewhat of a personal basis—yet it will seem outside of yourself until it happens to you. It is for this very reason that many women find it hard to pinpoint and call out. It is often covert, and we often feel that such behavior is so antiquated and farfetched that we experience a delayed reaction.

This brings us to the first antiquated bias that can leave us feeling caught off guard: gender bias. For those who aren't aware, this typically involves preconceived notions about the abilities, competence, and suitability of women in leadership positions. These preconceived notions are often negative or derogatory in nature and can undermine a female leader's authority. These biases can be centered around stereotypes that women are too emotional, indecisive, or lacking in assertiveness. Not only is this an issue in terms of the way in which female leaders are treated, and the apprehension they build up around trying not to exhibit these so-called "undesirable" qualities, but these biases can also lead to unfair evaluations and promotions.

Compounding general gender bias is intersectional bias, which can often significantly impact a woman's ability to really step into her leadership role and own it. Professor Deborah Gray White highlights why female leaders of color have historically been up against the ropes in terms of perception and biases, and her unpacking of this phenomenon is truly something to behold. In her insightful and honest exploration of the topic in her book, *Ar'n't I a Woman?: Female Slaves in the Plantation South* [6], Professor White states that as early as the emergence of chattel slavery, women of color have been yoked with the burdensome perception of being angry, loud, and abrupt. These are the very same qualities that might be perceived as assertive, strong, honest, or direct in a male leader. This narrative has been perpetuated ever since and has been used to try to subjugate women of color in leadership positions. Whether this has been overtly intentional or is a part of subconscious programming to view women of color in this light is, dare I say, irrelevant. What is really relevant is finding the means to identify it when it's happening, call it out, and find recourse. Now, even if you don't identify as a woman, it's important to take note of this because it could very well be impacting the women that you lead.

Experiencing racial and gender biases simultaneously makes it even more difficult for women to navigate their professional journeys. Addressing this issue and dismantling it is not an easy feat, nor is it something that should be the burden of female leaders to carry alone. It is something that needs to be brought to light, and those who perpetuate these negative stereotypes need to be held accountable. If not, the discrimination won't just stop at perceptions and side eyes around the water cooler. It can trickle down—or up—and leach into important decisions around pay and benefits. Yes, in this day and age, the gender pay gap still persists across industries and is particularly pronounced in leadership roles. Women may face challenges in negotiating fair compensation and encounter barriers when seeking advancement opportunities, further perpetuating inequalities. This is wrong on so many levels because, at the end of the day, no human being should ever feel that their identity as an individual is in any way tied to their job. Their personality should not be tied to scenarios of incitement, and their ability to do their job—and do it well—should not be linked to their gender or the color of their skin. When all is said and done, many women in leadership positions are there on a transactional basis. Their ability to earn and level up in that position should be hinged on the value that they provide the organization, and the organization should provide them with value in return. In any scenario where you are not legally seen as one with a business—such as the case might be for sole proprietors—you are not your job. Your ability to lead is not hinged on who you are but on who you embody within that role.

The problem is that those with oppositional views will say, "Just balance it." "Just balance your assertiveness with your likability." This is often referred to as the "double bind" phenomenon, which impacts women in all phases and areas of their lives. See if you can spot some of the double binds that you may have been subjected to in your life—or that you may have witnessed—by working through "Exercise 7: The Doubles that Bind."

The assertive-aggressive paradox that you'll also note through this comes up quite often because it has been used to shame women for being dominant in their roles. Women are often judged harshly if they display assertiveness and confidence, being labeled as "bossy" or "aggressive." Conversely, if they emphasize likability and nurturing qualities, they risk being perceived as someone who completely lacks leadership qualities. This double bind can create a challenging dynamic for women in leadership as they attempt to navigate the fine line between being effective leaders and conforming to societal expectations. On top of their mounting responsibilities as leaders, they are then faced with having to complete an intricate song and dance around getting people to approve of their leadership and who they are. While I would usually be a proponent for letting people feel how they are going to feel, it's not as easy when you're in a leadership role. To a certain degree, you need people to be **Team You** in order for you to lead them. This, in my opinion, is why women—especially women of color—get labeled as bad leaders in certain spheres. It's not because they lack the ability to lead. It is because people have perceptions of women that disable them from being led by a woman.

Addressing bias and discrimination requires both individual and systemic efforts. Leaders can build resilience by recognizing and challenging their own internalized biases and limiting beliefs. Seeking support networks, mentors, and allies who can provide guidance and advocacy is also crucial. Additionally, organizations need to implement diversity and inclusion initiatives with clear and enforceable policies. An organization that promotes equitable practices and provides training to raise awareness about unconscious bias and its impact will have more all-around success than those that don't.

How This Impacts Our Experiences

Intersectionality refers to the interconnected nature of social identities, such as race, gender, class, and more, and how they intersect to shape an individual's experiences and opportunities. When examining the experiences of women in leadership roles, it is crucial to consider intersectionality and its profound impact on their journeys. Intersectionality highlights the unique challenges and barriers that women face based on the convergence of their multiple identities.

Intersectionality recognizes that women's experiences are not uniform but are shaped by the interplay of various social categories. For example, women of color may face distinct challenges that differ from those faced by white women in leadership, as previously mentioned. Their experiences are shaped by both gender and race, resulting in a complex web of biases and discrimination. If this isn't addressed, this can quickly turn into the perfect storm for imposter syndrome to fester. This is because it's in our human makeup for our minds to play tricks on us. As you stand within some of the most demanding and, simultaneously, unfair phases of your life, you might find yourself thinking that if you were really meant to be there, it wouldn't be that hard for you to assimilate, fit in, or adapt to the role. Don't do this to yourself. Don't get into that frame of mind because it is the environment around you that is having a hard time adapting to you, and that has absolutely nothing—and I mean nothing—to do with you or your abilities.

If you find yourself experiencing stereotypes and prejudices that stereotype you as less competent or qualified compared to your white counterparts, do your level best to call it out. Even if your voice quivers and even if it feels like you shouldn't have to be doing that—because you shouldn't. These biases can undermine your credibility and limit your opportunities for career advancement, so you need to be able to use your voice and call a spade a spade.

The real issue is that the experience of intersectional bias doesn't just provide female leaders with another mental hurdle to contend with, it also limits their access to resources and opportunities. If, for instance, you happen to be a woman who is perceived as coming from a lower socioeconomic background, the intersections of gender and class can create additional barriers. Economic disparities, lack of access to quality education and networking opportunities, and systemic disadvantages can impede your progress in leadership roles. Let's be clear that there are levels to this unfortunate circumstance of the world we live in. There is true networking and having access to information about opportunities in wider circles, and then there is plain nepotism. That is not what I'm referring to or supporting here. That said, when you only have to walk in a straight line toward a goal, such as a leadership role, without having to zig-zag around socioeconomic hurdles, it does make things a little easier. Overcoming anything in the range of a lack of access to certain circles as well as financial constraints in a bid to navigate environments that already do not prioritize diversity and inclusion is a major problem.

Then, there are the experiences of LGBTQ+ women in leadership. These women's experiences are also influenced by intersectionality. These women face unique challenges due to the combination of their sexual orientation or gender identity and existing gender-based biases. They may encounter prejudice, stereotypes, and discrimination, which can impact their sense of belonging and opportunities for advancement. The intersection of gender and LGBTQ+ identity brings forth additional complexities that need to be recognized and addressed.

This brings us back to the stereotype that women are emotional or angry beings by nature. If we were to run down this entire list of possible biases and impose them on our male counterparts, they might find themselves in a position where they were at least a little temperamental from time to time. They would have every reason to be. After all, we could say that life had handed them so many lemons that they would be practically drowning in the stuff. However, women are not allowed to be angry at injustice. We're not allowed to say, "You know what, that's just not right." If we do, we're labeled as angry, venomous, and cold. What's worse is that the majority of the time, we're not actually exhibiting that level of anger, despite the fact that we should. All we're doing is asking for a little respect and acknowledgment.

Intersectionality calls for an inclusive and holistic approach to leadership development. It emphasizes the importance of creating spaces where all women can thrive, regardless of their intersecting identities. Organizations need to foster inclusive cultures, recognize and celebrate diversity, and ensure that policies and practices promote equity and fairness. Yes, these weren't always topics that were high up on the agenda of corporate or organizational affairs, but now that we know better collectively, we need to do better.

We can't just brush this aside any longer.

Recognizing Toxicity & Calling It Out

We looked at how difficult it can be to call out toxic behavior in the workplace, even if you're in a leadership role, and it's important that we discuss this now. I will point out that it's not often the people you lead who undermine your leadership but those alongside you.

If you're a marketing manager, for example, you might find that the sales manager or the head of accounting creates problems for you in the workplace. There are countless cases where women come into organizations with nothing but the best intentions, a smile, and a can-do attitude, only to be shut down by the people who should be welcoming them. A cycle of snide remarks and backbiting can occur, and when confronted about all of this, you might find yourself in a position of being gaslit.

Gaslighting is a harmful manipulation tactic that involves undermining someone's perceptions, beliefs, and experiences to make them doubt their own reality. Unfortunately, gaslighting is a phenomenon that can be experienced by female leaders in the workplace, perpetuated more commonly by fellow team leaders—as mentioned. This behavior can have detrimental effects on your confidence, credibility, and overall well-being.

One way in which fellow team leaders may gaslight women leaders is by dismissing or downplaying their ideas and contributions. This can involve taking credit for their work, diminishing their achievements, or disregarding their input during decision-making processes. By undermining the value and significance of their contributions, gaslighting team leaders aim to erode the confidence and self-assurance of fellow leaders who so happen to be female. It's important for you to see these people for what they are. At the risk of generalizing, these people are often insecure and feel the need to downplay your abilities in a bid to safeguard themselves from some self-construed catastrophic idea of what might happen if you "outshine" them.

In other words, they think you're going to get them passed up for a promotion or, worse, fired. Instead of seeing your abilities as a beacon, which can help the organization flourish, or a form of encouragement to do better, they see you as a threat.

Gaslighting may also manifest in the form of subtle or overt criticism and belittlement. Fellow team leaders may use derogatory language, make demeaning comments, or engage in subtle acts of sabotage to undermine the authority and credibility of female leaders. This behavior serves to create self-doubt and make them question their abilities and qualifications. If you find yourself in a position such as this, practicing the repeat is one way to tackle the problem. This involves a process of repeating someone's statement and then asking them if you've repeated it correctly. For instance, "So, you're saying that the success of this entire project was a result of some stroke of luck and is not an indication of my abilities, and thus my deservedness to be team leader—is that correct?" Hearing their own words and knowing that you've processed exactly what they have said is enough to make them feel uncomfortable. This is not something they'll likely want to experience again and, in most cases, this will be the end of the road for their behavior. With all of this in mind, try to be aware that certain tactics, such as this, can feel passive-aggressive. If you're not careful about how you deploy these tactics and how they make you feel in post, it could lead to degradation of your own habits and behavior. People might invite you to the crazy party, but you don't have to attend.

Another way in which gaslighting can occur is through the invalidation of emotions and experiences. If, for example, there is someone higher than you up the chain of command and you would like to seek their advice on your interaction with Person X that we just discussed, you might face gaslighting there too. It is not uncommon that when you express your concerns or frustrations, gaslighting team leaders may dismiss your feelings, label you as overly sensitive, or suggest that you are overreacting. For some reason, if a man expresses concern over such behavior, it is met with support or, at the very least, an "I'll look into it." When women do it, they're often met with, "Are you sure that's what they meant?" Now, don't get me wrong, that question is not always rooted in ill intent. It's often an attempt to keep the peace and not rock the boat. This invalidation of emotions can, nonetheless, make you question your perceptions and hesitate to address the issues you face in the future. This lack of support is like kindling for imposter syndrome. When you're in a position to doubt your experiences, it's all too easy to begin doubting everything else about yourself.

If your higher-ups aren't unintentionally gaslighting you, they might be on the opposite end of the spectrum as they attempt to manipulate power dynamics. They may use their authority to exert control, intimidate, or create a hostile environment for you. People like this are difficult to deal with. By leveraging their position, they aim to maintain a sense of superiority and assert dominance over their female counterparts, further eroding their confidence and ability to lead effectively. Knowing the difference between a situation you can withstand (or alter) and one that is simply going to prevent you from gaining any actual experience is key. You cannot save every organization from the rot that impedes its growth.

The impact of gaslighting is significant and will be detrimental to your mental health. How long that detriment is felt all depends on how long you allow it to affect you. Your options, as with anything else in this life, are to change the situation or walk away from it. If the organization cannot find a way to foster a culture of respect, empathy, and inclusion to address the issue of gaslighting—especially if you've given them the time and the advice on how you believe this could be done—it might be time to find other opportunities. If the organization is serious about retaining high-caliber leaders, or if you have the authority to institute change—then leadership training programs can be implemented to emphasize the importance of respectful communication, active listening, and valuing diverse perspectives. Creating a safe space for female leaders to express their concerns and providing support systems, such as mentors or coaches, can help counteract the effects of gaslighting.

Calling this behavior out, however, will always be the best route to remedying the issue at its core. While we've already looked at tactics such as "repeat & clarify," there are other means for calling out toxic behavior. You can explore them in "Exercise 8: Calling Out Toxic Workplace Behavior" in your accompanying workbook.

Nonetheless, navigating bias and discrimination in the workplace requires practical tools and strategies to overcome these challenges. Two effective approaches are allyship and mentorship.

Allyship involves individuals, regardless of their background, actively supporting and advocating for marginalized colleagues. Allies listen, educate themselves, and use their privilege to challenge biases and promote equity. They create a safe space for open conversations, amplify marginalized voices, and work toward inclusive policies and practices. By fostering an environment of trust and support, allyship helps combat bias and discrimination.

Mentorship plays a crucial role in empowering individuals to navigate bias and discrimination. Mentors provide guidance, share experiences, and offer career advice to help their mentees overcome challenges. They can help identify and address biases in the workplace, provide strategies for navigating difficult situations, and offer networking opportunities. Mentors can also support their mentees in building self-confidence and resilience, helping them thrive despite potential obstacles. Finally, they can reassure them that what they are experiencing is a legitimate cause for concern and that they are not being overly emotional.

To implement allyship and mentorship effectively, organizations should provide training and resources to raise awareness about bias and discrimination. This training can educate employees about different forms of bias, the impact of discrimination, and how to be effective allies and mentors. It is important to note that allyship and mentorship are ever-evolving processes that are long-term commitments. Building authentic relationships, continuous learning, and active engagement are key to combatting bias and discrimination effectively, and these are not one-off events. However, it is so worth it because by embracing these practical tools, individuals and organizations can create positive change and foster a more equitable workplace for everyone.

*

Once you've walked the road of acknowledging your own imposter syndrome and you've worked hard to assure yourself of your own abilities, having it all dashed away by someone else is a painful blow. This is especially true if this is someone that you have to face on a near-daily basis and within your leadership role. With a little more know-how on how to navigate this difficult period, we can begin focusing on building more positivity in your life. We'll begin with your self-confidence as a matter of priority next.

JB

CHAPTER 10
BUILDING SELF-CONFIDENCE

Building self-confidence is a vital aspect of personal and professional growth, particularly for leaders who may face unique challenges in navigating their roles. Confidence empowers leaders to express their ideas, make decisions, and lead with conviction. However, self-confidence is not an inherent trait but rather a skill that can be developed and nurtured over time. That is fantastic news for anyone who is suffering from self-doubt and imposter syndrome.

This chapter focuses on the journey of building self-confidence as a leader. We will explore the underlying factors, obstacles, and strategies that contribute to cultivating a strong sense of self-assurance. By understanding the importance of self-confidence and the specific context in which modern-day leaders operate, we can embark on a transformative path toward greater self-belief and empowerment. Not only that, but we will also delve into the dynamics of self-confidence, exploring how it impacts leadership effectiveness and the ability to navigate the complexities of the modern workplace. By acknowledging the challenges that many leaders face, we can gain insight into the underlying issues that may hinder self-confidence and begin to address them.

Finally, we will get into the benefits of stepping out of your comfort zone and learning to reframe your point of view. These two elements will be unbelievably pivotal in changing the way you see yourself and the world around you.

Through personal research insights and practical strategies, this chapter aims to empower leaders to embark on a journey of self-discovery and self-empowerment. By embracing the process of building self-confidence and recognizing that it is a continuous journey, we can unlock our true potential, overcome self-doubt, and cultivate a strong sense of self-belief that propels us forward in our leadership roles.

We begin with milestones in your life that truly matter.

Milestones That Matter

Building self-confidence is an essential journey for people in leadership roles as it enables them to overcome self-doubt and imposter syndrome. Being able to embrace one's true capabilities can truly offer a new lease on life. While building self-confidence is a deeply personal and individual process, there are several effective tips and strategies that can support its development.

The first step is to set achievable goals. Setting realistic and attainable goals provides a sense of direction and accomplishment. By breaking larger objectives into smaller, manageable tasks, you can build confidence through a series of small victories. Celebrating each milestone along the way reinforces a sense of progress and boosts self-assurance. It's important to note that breaking your goal down into smaller goals isn't supposed to overwhelm you. You shouldn't feel like you have a million things to get through, and if you do, the odds are that you've set the deadline for your big goal too close. Imagine it this way. If you have a goal that requires you to complete one hundred milestones on the way to achieving it, you're going to feel overwhelmed if you set your deadline for next weekend. On the other hand, if you're realistic and set your deadline for this time next year, you'll have twelve months to accomplish all of the preceding milestones. That's an average of eight milestones to complete each month or two to complete each week. I don't know about you, but completing two milestones by next week sounds a lot more doable than completing one hundred by next week. Ultimately, try to be aware of what will burn you out and what won't. Then, strive to strike a balance and focus on maintaining your self-care.

    Practicing self-care is arguably one of the most vital aspects of building self-confidence. As discussed in Chapter 6, taking care of one's physical, mental, and emotional well-being lays a strong foundation for self-assurance and a sense of self-love. Engaging in activities that promote relaxation, such as exercise, mindfulness, or hobbies, nurtures self-esteem and resilience. Additionally, establishing healthy boundaries and prioritizing self-care helps prevent burnout and promotes overall confidence and well-being. When you feel good about yourself, and you make a mental, concerted effort to take care of your well-being, you're unwittingly telling yourself that you're worth all of that effort... and then some! Remember, what you feed your brain is what it will believe. Therefore, the more you practice self-care, the more confident you become.

Another one of the most effective strategies for regaining a sense of self-confidence is to challenge those negative thoughts that trickle into your mind throughout the day and replace them with positivity. Negative self-talk often feeds self-doubt and undermines confidence. By identifying and reframing negative thoughts, you can cultivate a more positive and empowering inner dialogue. You can head back to **Exercise 3** in your workbook for a reminder of how affirmations work and how you can create your own.

Using affirmations and self-care as lubricants for the rough roads that lay ahead on your way to hitting your milestones is an essential part of the process. This will allow you to move from success to success. Celebrating successes, no matter how small, is an essential practice for building self-confidence. Recognizing and acknowledging your achievements will reinforce a positive self-image and reinforce belief in your capabilities. Whether it's completing a project or receiving positive feedback, taking the time to celebrate and appreciate your accomplishments is a guaranteed boost in motivation.

Once you have a handle on this, you can explore the world beyond the boundaries of your comfort zone.

Stepping Out of Your Comfort Zone

Stepping out of your comfort zone requires an unparalleled level of self-confidence. But how do you do it? How do you go from maintaining a consistent routine and thriving in predictability to rocking the boat?

Those are good questions, and here is the answer.

You start by saying, "Yes." You say yes to things that you would usually say no to. They don't have to be things that cause you to flout your morals or values. Similarly, they shouldn't be things that make you feel uneasy in your own skin. They should, however, be things that push the boundaries of your comfort zone. For inspiration on how to achieve this, head to Exercise 9 in your workbook.

When you're able to break out of your shell and embrace the unknown, it will be easier for you to take the next step of shifting your perspective.

Why You Should Shift Your Perspective

Shifting your perspective is crucial for overcoming imposter syndrome as it allows you to challenge and change the negative thought patterns and self-perceptions that contribute to feeling like a fraud. By shifting your perspective, you can gain a more accurate and balanced view of yourself and your abilities, thus leading to increased self-confidence and a reduction in imposter feelings.

One key reason why shifting your perspective is important is that it helps you reframe your accomplishments and recognize your true worth. Imposter syndrome often causes individuals to undermine their achievements, dismissing them as insignificant or undeserved. By shifting your perspective, you can acknowledge your accomplishments as valid and recognize the effort, skills, and strengths that contributed to your success. This shift in perspective allows you to embrace a more positive and realistic self-assessment, thus boosting your confidence and helping you see yourself as capable and competent.

The question is, how do you shift your perspective?

How do you recognize your accomplishments when your brain is already telling you that they're worthless?

For starters, you can reach out to past mentors, professors, colleagues, and employers. Remember that more goodness grows outside of your comfort zone than within it . . . and get vulnerable. Be honest about what you're experiencing, and let them know that you're just looking for some insight into how they perceived you during their time with you. Just like getting comfortable with seeing yourself through the lens of a camera (or hearing yourself on a voice recording), you'll use this external perspective to shift your own.

This can help you challenge the unrealistic expectations and comparisons that fuel imposter syndrome. Many individuals suffering from imposter feelings set unattainable standards for themselves and constantly compare themselves to others, leading to a sense of inadequacy and self-doubt. Becoming more introspective allows you to focus on your journey and the trajectory of your growth. This shift allows you to appreciate your individual strengths and recognize that everyone has their own path and set of challenges. It enables you to embrace self-acceptance and recognize that you are enough as you are.

Another important aspect of shifting your perspective is developing a mindset of self-compassion. Imposter syndrome often involves self-criticism, harsh judgment, and fear of failure. By shifting your perspective, you can cultivate self-compassion, which involves treating yourself with a sense of kindness, understanding, and empathy. This shift allows you to respond to self-doubt and setbacks with self-care. It also allows you to engage in self-support rather than self-criticism. Plus, it helps you develop resilience in the face of challenges and fosters a more nurturing and empowering relationship with yourself. To become more self-compassionate, you can:

- **Listen to your body.** When you're in a state of panic, ask yourself why. Try to get to the root, and when you do, assure yourself that the situation will pass. Speak kindly to yourself as you would a young child who is frightened. Self-soothe, and if the situation really calls for it, treat yourself to something that makes you feel better. Just try not to create a vice out of it.

- **Become more self-reliant.** When you've received the external validation that you need, try not to seek it out on a regular basis. Instead, learn how to tell yourself that you are worthy and whole as you are.

Shifting your perspective involves focusing on personal growth and learning rather than seeking external validation. While this is something that you can initially do to placate yourself, you need to focus within. Imposter syndrome often stems from a constant need for approval and validation from others, leading to a never-ending cycle of seeking reassurance. By shifting your perspective, you can prioritize your own growth and development. Focus on acquiring new skills, expanding your knowledge, and embracing continuous learning. This will help you derive fulfillment and satisfaction from personal growth rather than solely relying on external validation, thus reducing the grip of imposter feelings.

It all comes down to perspective shifting.

How to Reframe Your POV

Perspective-shifting strategies are powerful tools for overcoming imposter syndrome and building self-confidence. They help to:

- Challenge negative thoughts and beliefs,
- Reframe situations in a more positive light, and,
- Cultivate a mindset of self-belief and self-empowerment.

The three most effective perspective-shifting strategies in my experience are reframing thoughts, visualization, and positive self-talk.

Reframing thoughts involves consciously examining and replacing negative or self-limiting thoughts with more positive and empowering ones. We already looked at this in Chapter 6, so I won't go into it in too much detail here. I will add to it by saying this: When experiencing imposter feelings, individuals tend to focus on their perceived shortcomings and failures. Reframing allows you to challenge and change these thoughts by questioning their accuracy and providing alternative interpretations.

Visualization is a powerful technique that involves creating vivid mental images of yourself succeeding, being confident, and feeling empowered. By visualizing positive outcomes and seeing yourself as capable and successful, you can reshape your self-perception and boost your confidence. Visualization helps to rewire the brain and build a sense of belief in your abilities. Take a few moments each day to visualize yourself achieving your goals, leading with confidence, and overcoming challenges. Engage all your senses and immerse yourself in the positive emotions associated with your visualized success.

Then, we have a controversial tool for reframing your POV: arguing with yourself. By actively arguing with the negative thoughts in your mind, you can become defensive over the inner child and inner leader who is under attack. It's important to use this sparingly and not too in-depth because, if prolonged, it can lead to heightened levels of anger.

It's important to note that these strategies are not one-time fixes but require consistent practice and effort. Incorporating them into your daily routine can gradually rewire your thought patterns and help you develop a more empowering mindset. The key to making this work is finding what suits you the best. You have to consciously engage with the strategies that you decide on in order for this to work. But remember to be patient with yourself and practice self-compassion as you navigate the process of shifting your perspective.

*

We are nearing the final tips, tools, and techniques for overcoming imposter syndrome while taking on a leadership role, and your mindset should be shifting at this point. Now, we're going to change gears as we dive into the benefits of vulnerability in overcoming imposter syndrome.

JB

CHAPTER 11
THE POWER OF VULNERABILITY

Leaders are increasingly recognizing the power of vulnerability in creating meaningful connections, fostering trust, and driving success. Being a vulnerable leader means embracing authenticity, openness, and the willingness to show one's true self, including acknowledging fears, limitations, and uncertainties. By breaking down the walls of perfection and invulnerability, leaders can tap into a powerful force that transcends traditional notions of leadership. Brené Brown perhaps said it best: "The courage to be vulnerable is not about winning or losing, it's about the courage to show up when you can't predict or control the outcome." [7]

That's a powerful message because part of imposter syndrome lies in the fear of unpredictability. When we're unable to predict how people will judge us or how they'll react if we fail (or aren't as perfect as we'd like them to think), we freeze. Vulnerability is, therefore, such a powerful act of love—love for the self, the team, and the organization.

The true power of being vulnerable lies in its ability to create a transformative and inclusive work environment. When leaders have the courage to show vulnerability, they set the tone for others to do the same. It creates a space where team members feel safe to express their thoughts, share their challenges, and contribute their unique perspectives. This environment of trust and psychological safety cultivates collaboration, creativity, and innovation. These three elements are the cornerstones of practically any organization.

What's more, vulnerability in leadership fosters empathy and understanding. When leaders are open about their own struggles and setbacks, they build deeper connections with their team members. This empathy enables leaders to better understand the needs and emotions of their team, leading to improved communication, stronger relationships, and a more supportive work culture. Embracing vulnerability as a leader allows for personal and professional growth because acknowledging and learning from mistakes allows leaders to model a growth mindset. This, in turn, encourages continuous learning, improvement, and resilience. Ultimately, this vulnerability creates a culture where experimentation and calculated risks are celebrated, leading to new discoveries, breakthrough ideas, and the ability to adapt to change. The difference between an organization built on fear and one built on vulnerability and acceptance is night and day.

Throughout this chapter, we will delve into the power of being a vulnerable leader and explore its impact on individuals, teams, and organizations. This vulnerability will enhance your leadership effectiveness and create a positive as well as empowering workplace environment. By embracing vulnerability, you can tap into your authentic self, inspire others, and drive meaningful change in your organizations and beyond.

So, let's begin.

Leave No Stone Unturned

When you're vulnerable, there is no stone that anyone can turn to shake you or make you seem like a bad leader. When you are honest and candid, there is nothing left to hide. More importantly, there is nothing that anyone can use against you. This is the beauty that lies in self-acceptance and vulnerability.

In the realm of leadership, there is an undeniable strength that comes from embracing authenticity and practicing transparency. When you lead with honesty and candor, you create a solid foundation of trust and credibility, both within yourself and among those you lead.

But what is authenticity if not some overused buzzword?

Authenticity is about being true to yourself and aligning your actions, values, and beliefs. It involves embracing your unique strengths, vulnerabilities, and experiences, as well as bringing your genuine self to your leadership role. When you lead authentically, you project an aura of confidence and inspire others to do the same. By staying true to your principles, you cultivate a sense of trust and authenticity in your interactions with others, thus fostering an environment where people feel safe. This is a feeling of safety to express themselves, contribute their ideas, and collaborate effectively. Part of this involves being open about your own mistakes and flaws. You might even benefit from being honest about your own struggles with self-doubt. You may very well open the floodgates on a conversation with those in your team who toil with the very same internal struggle.

It all comes down to being transparent, and transparency goes hand in hand with authenticity since it involves open and honest communication. When you are transparent, you willingly share information, provide clarity on your decisions and actions, and foster an environment of openness as well as trust. Transparency enables you to build strong connections with your team and stakeholders because it demonstrates that you have nothing to hide and that you value and respect their perspectives. By being transparent, you create a space where everyone feels informed, included, and empowered.

More importantly, you create an environment where everyone feels seen.

My earlier statement on leaving no stone that anyone can turn to shake you or make you seem like a bad leader speaks to the resilience that comes from leading with authenticity and transparency. However, it also speaks to your ability to remain constant in uncertain situations. When you consistently embody these qualities, you are not easily swayed or undermined by external criticism or attempts to discredit your leadership. Your authenticity serves as a shield, protecting you from doubt, insecurity, and negative judgment. By being open and honest, you leave no room for assumptions, rumors, or hidden agendas, thus eradicating potential ammunition that others may use against you.

Finally, when you are honest and candid, you create an environment of trust and psychological safety. People appreciate leaders who are forthright and transparent because it allows them to have a clear understanding of expectations, decisions, and strategies. That takes so much of the edge off in an already competitive or high-powered work setting because no one is left second-guessing where they stand. There is no confusion as to what they should be doing or how management perceives them. This transparency encourages open dialogue and constructive feedback. It fosters a culture where mistakes can be acknowledged and learned from without fear of retribution or blame. By embracing transparency, you encourage others to follow suit, thus building a culture of accountability and authenticity throughout your organization.

With all that said, I truly do understand how embracing vulnerability can be difficult. This is why I've dedicated the next subchapter to learning how to do so.

Learning How to Embrace Vulnerability

Vulnerability is often misunderstood as a sign of weakness or a lack of confidence. However, it is quite the opposite. Embracing vulnerability means acknowledging and accepting our imperfections, limitations, and insecurities—and allowing ourselves to be seen authentically. For leaders who may face societal expectations of always being strong and having to have all the answers to avoid being seen as "overly emotional," embracing vulnerability can be transformative in overcoming imposter syndrome. This is because vulnerability allows us to establish genuine connections with others. When we open up about our struggles, fears, and self-doubt, we create a space for empathy, understanding, and support. Sharing our vulnerabilities with trusted colleagues, mentors, or support networks helps us realize that we are not alone in our experiences. It fosters a sense of camaraderie and allows others to provide guidance, reassurance, and perspective. To dive into the process by which you can embrace vulnerability, please head to "Exercise 10: Leaning into Vulnerability" in your accompanying workbook.

Now, I want to get something off my chest. If you consider yourself quite traditional in terms of your leadership and you think that vulnerability is just new-age "mumbo jumbo," you'd be dead wrong. It takes a great deal of strength and courage to open up in this way, and organizations that have embraced this have grown in strength. Even leaders who were once self-proclaimed stoics who doggedly drove their teams, like Steve Jobs and Bill Gates, eventually admitted to the power of modern leadership techniques. Allow me to introduce you to some incredible leaders who have brought their vulnerability into the spotlight.

Vulnerable Leaders in Spotlight

Throughout history, there have been numerous individuals who have embraced vulnerability as a powerful tool to achieve their goals. By stepping into their vulnerability, they have defied societal norms, overcome obstacles, and made a significant impact in their respective fields. For starters, we'll come back to Brené Brown—a renowned research professor, author, and speaker. She has dedicated her work to exploring the paradigms of vulnerability, courage, and shame. She has shared her vulnerabilities and struggles openly, encouraging others to embrace their own as a source of strength. Through her TED Talks and books like *Daring Greatly* and *The Power of Vulnerability*, she has inspired millions to shed their armor, cultivate authenticity, and live wholeheartedly.

And living wholeheartedly is something that our next vulnerable leader (one who has previously featured in this book) has showcased throughout her life. As one of the greatest tennis players of all time, Serena Williams has not only showcased her exceptional skills on the court but also her vulnerability and resilience. She has openly discussed the challenges she has faced, both in her personal life and in her career. Her honest essay [8] that delved into her post-childbirth experience in 2017 has shed light on the plight that many women of color face post-birth. While she admits that her own circumstances were not as harrowing as they could have been if she had not been listened to by medical staff, she knew that raising awareness about the matter was crucial for those who might not have the good fortune. But this wasn't the only time that Williams has shown us that vulnerability. She has shown us that honest conversations are needed throughout all areas of life. By constantly embracing vulnerability and acknowledging her fears and insecurities, she has been able to bounce back from setbacks on the court and has inspired others to do the same. She fearlessly raised her voice for those who can't.

This is something that Malala Yousafzai is no stranger to as she continues to advocate for girls' education and women's rights despite facing life-threatening adversity. Her unwavering courage and vulnerability in sharing her own story of surviving an attack by the Taliban have empowered countless girls and women worldwide to stand up for themselves in the face of seemingly impossible odds. Malala's vulnerability has been instrumental in breaking down barriers, challenging societal norms, and driving global change.

These examples illustrate how embracing vulnerability can lead to remarkable achievements. By sharing their vulnerabilities and being open about their fears, insecurities, and setbacks, these individuals have inspired millions to embrace their own vulnerabilities, take risks, and pursue their goals with authenticity and determination, no matter what the cost.

*

Being vulnerable will set you and those around you free from unrealistic expectations and the need to please others. When you give yourself the grace and space to be an actual human being, there is little else that can stand in the way of your success. This is because when you realize that we're all **real** and that we all bleed, you'll begin to see how fleeting and impermanent life is. You'll also begin to understand that we were made to share in each other's lives as authentically as possible, not to strive for perfection.

In my opinion, there is no such thing.

Accepting this will allow you to better embrace intuition in the workplace.

JB

CHAPTER 12
ALLOWING INTUITION TO BE YOUR GUIDE IN THE WORKPLACE

Navigating self-doubt and imposter syndrome in the workplace can be a challenging journey, but sometimes the most valuable guidance we have is within ourselves: our intuition. This chapter explores the power of trusting your gut and listening to your inner voice as you navigate the complex landscape of self-doubt and imposter syndrome.

Our gut feelings, often referred to as intuition, are a powerful tool that can provide invaluable insights and guidance. They arise from a combination of our subconscious mind processing subtle cues and patterns that our conscious mind may not immediately recognize. Our gut feelings can act as an internal compass, guiding us toward decisions and actions that align with our authentic selves.

Trusting your gut becomes particularly important when faced with self-doubt and imposter syndrome in the workplace. These challenges can cloud our judgment and make it difficult to discern our true capabilities and worth. In such moments, our intuition can help cut through the noise and offer a clearer perspective. By tapping into our inner wisdom, we can find the strength to make choices that align with our true potential.

As we progress, we will explore the significance of trusting your gut, as well as how to cultivate a deeper connection with your intuition and the ways in which it can empower you to navigate self-doubt and imposter syndrome. We will delve into the reasons why your intuition is a reliable guide, even when it may defy logic or external expectations. You will discover how trusting your gut can lead to greater self-awareness, confidence, and success in the face of adversity.

How Self-Doubt Impacts Our Careers

As you now know, these psychological phenomena can undermine confidence, hinder growth, and limit opportunities for professional advancement. Understanding the impact of self-doubt and imposter syndrome is crucial for empowering leaders to overcome these challenges and thrive in leadership roles.

One of the significant ways self-doubt and imposter syndrome can affect a leader's career is by diminishing their confidence. When plagued by self-doubt, leaders may question their abilities, qualifications, and worthiness of their positions. This lack of confidence can lead to a reluctance to take on new challenges, express ideas, or seek promotions.

As a result, opportunities for career advancement may be missed, and you may remain in roles below your true potential. Outside of the employee lane, there are entrepreneurs who refuse to raise pricing for their services out of the fear that they are not worthy of those rates and will, therefore, price themselves out of a market that is more in line with their assumed "speed." They miss out on high-ticket clients in a bid to keep themselves busy with a multitude of mid-level projects. While there is nothing inherently wrong with this, the human spirit craves progress. If we didn't, we would still be hunkered down in a cave, fighting off predators and painting the day's events on the walls. When we're caught in a rut that is completely devoid of all progress, we feel as though life has no meaning. That, in itself, is enough to send anyone on a downward spiral on both a mental and emotional front.

For the leader who is already struggling with imposter syndrome, this can lead to self-sabotaging behaviors, such as avoiding visibility or feeling overwhelmed by the fear of being exposed as incompetent.

Consequently, you may not fully contribute your talents because of the idea that if you only give 50% of yourself to something and it goes wrong at least you can subconsciously assure yourself that it wasn't your "all" that was up for review anyway. At the end of the day, you can't get shot down if you're not fully in the game.

When a person undervalues their worth as a leader and hesitates to advocate for themselves, it can impact the way they navigate leadership challenges and assert their authority. The fear of being perceived in an unforgiving light can lead to self-censorship. That is a nightmare waiting to happen for everyone involved. Leaders are still human beings with lives beyond the frontlines of their organizations. Self-censorship will, over time, lead to a loss of one's sense of self. There is no leadership role on the face of this earth that is worth losing yourself over. While there is a huge difference between losing yourself over a specific role and losing yourself due to your own experience with imposter syndrome, you'll have to address it either way.

Just to try to keep in mind that while these effects of self-doubt and imposter syndrome are not exclusive to leaders, the social and cultural dynamics in the workplace can exacerbate their impact on those at the helm.

The good news is that we're steadily unpacking ways to deal with it all.

Dealing with Self-Doubt in the Workplace

As mentioned, embracing intuition (our innate and instinctual sense) is a powerful approach to combat imposter syndrome. It allows us to tap into our inner wisdom, gaining clarity when faced with self-doubt. By connecting with our intuition, we can make choices that align with our authentic selves, thus facilitating personal and professional growth. This is important because, despite the noise of imposter syndrome, your gut's low and genuine vibration will tell you otherwise. You just have to be silent and emotionally centered for long enough to pick up on it.

This brings us right back to the importance of self-awareness, which is crucial for overcoming imposter syndrome and harnessing the power of intuition. Through mindfulness practices like meditation or journaling, we cultivate self-awareness. This is predominantly done by observing our thoughts, emotions, and triggers. This practice enables us to identify patterns of self-doubt and negative self-talk that perpetuate imposter syndrome. By exploring the underlying causes of our insecurities, we can challenge irrational beliefs and separate fact from fiction. This is an essential practice because to trust your gut, you need to know that it is, indeed, your intuition speaking to you and not just negative brain chatter.

Negative self-talk plays a significant role in perpetuating imposter syndrome. When self-deprecating statements arise, we can question their validity by examining the evidence that supports or contradicts them. Knowing that you have a negative inner voice will help you circumnavigate it without being misled into believing that it is your intuition. You'll be able to acknowledge it for what it is and bypass it on your way to retrieving true information about yourself when you are in a calmer frame of mind. I've spoken about dysregulation and being calm on several occasions now, and the reason for this is that imposter syndrome very seldom rears its head when the going is good. It's in the moments when the going is really tough that it decides to waltz into your mind and take up root. So, it goes without saying that it is in those chaotic, panic-infused, dysregulated moments that you will need these techniques the most.

If you can move past the initial discomfort that the onset of imposter syndrome symptoms present, you can find a positive way of dealing with the real scenario that is in front of you—not the hyperinflated one that the negative inner voice has painted for you. Cultivating a positive mindset is crucial for overcoming imposter syndrome and building self-confidence. Gratitude practices of any kind will contribute to a more positive outlook. Therefore, whatever fills your cup with more gratitude, do more of that!

This will help you to fix and trust your gut. For more steps on how to do this, head to "Exercise 11: Fixing & Trusting Your Gut" in your accompanying workbook now. From there, you can set your sights on your allies.

Knowing Who Your Allies Are

When building a support network, it's crucial to recognize that not everyone can be trusted, and sometimes our alarm bells are justified. While cultivating a strong support system is essential for personal and professional growth, it is equally important to exercise caution and discernment when selecting individuals to include in our network. Trusting the wrong people can have negative consequences. It can erode self-confidence, exacerbate self-doubt, and increase feelings of imposter syndrome. Therefore, it's essential to be mindful of the potential risks and employ strategies to protect ourselves from those who may not have our best interests at heart.

First, it's important to listen to your intuition and pay attention to your instincts. Your gut feelings are often valuable indicators that shouldn't be dismissed lightly. If something feels off, it probably is. Try to take a step back and evaluate the situation for what it is. Your subconscious mind can pick up on subtle cues and patterns that your conscious mind may not immediately recognize. Trusting your instincts can help you avoid potential harm and ensure that you surround yourself with individuals who genuinely support and uplift you.

    Another important factor in building a reliable support network is to conduct due diligence and assess the people you are considering letting in before fully trusting them. This can involve researching their backgrounds, seeking recommendations or references, and observing their behavior and interactions with others. Taking the time to gather information and gain insights into their character can help you make informed decisions about who to include in your network. Just beware not to come across as someone who is trying to pry into the life of another person. There is enough to deal with regarding imposter syndrome; we don't need you to come across as the office gossip on top of the immense weight you're likely already carrying. So, as a final word on the subject, do your digging when the time calls for it, but don't be overtly distrusting of people who haven't given you a reason not to trust them.

    To truly figure out who your allies are in the workplace, try to cultivate relationships gradually and allow trust to develop over time. Building allyships is not a race but a journey. By gradually opening up and sharing personal and professional experiences, you can gauge how others respond and whether they demonstrate genuine empathy and support. Rushing into deep trust can leave you prematurely vulnerable and susceptible to manipulation or exploitation. Taking the time to establish a foundation of trust helps ensure that you are building relationships with individuals who are dependable and reliable.

In addition, seeking diverse perspectives and feedback is crucial when developing a support network. Surrounding yourself with people who challenge you, provide constructive criticism, and offer different viewpoints will help you grow and make better-informed decisions. It's important to value diversity of thought and surround yourself with individuals who encourage independent thinking rather than simply seeking validation or agreement. Doing this will bolster the fact that you've found the right ally because you'll know that their support of your plights is not fake.

As you form these relationships in the workplace, maintaining healthy boundaries will be essential. Not everyone needs access to the intimate details of your life. Setting clear boundaries around the type and level of information you share will help to protect your emotional well-being and maintain a healthy balance in your relationships. It's important to remember that trust is earned, and it is perfectly acceptable to be selective about the level of trust you place in others. All you need to stay aware of is your delivery because a boundary is a loving perimeter we set up as an honor to ourselves, not an angry electric fence meant to shock and hurt anyone who dares come near it.

*

Navigating imposter syndrome at work is one of the more difficult tasks that you will grapple with where this phenomenon is concerned. However, it can affect your personal life too. As mentioned, you don't exist in a vacuum, and your personal life can have just as profound of an impact on your leadership abilities as your work life can have on your ability to maintain a healthy personal life. I would be remiss not to touch on this, and this is why we're heading down this road next.

JB

CHAPTER 13
OVERCOMING SELF-DOUBT AND IMPOSTER SYNDROME IN PERSONAL RELATIONSHIPS

In our personal relationships, self-doubt and imposter syndrome can also find a way to creep in. Each can significantly impact our well-being and connections with others. Whether you're struggling with imposter syndrome on a professional level and that stress is impacting your relationship or you feel like an imposter within your relationship itself, this is something that should be addressed before it spirals. If it isn't addressed, it can create barriers to intimacy, a lack of vulnerability, and a rise in inauthentic communication. Before we delve further into this chapter, it's important to look at how the phenomena can manifest in a personal relationship.

Self-doubt and imposter syndrome can manifest in various ways within personal relationships. Individuals may question their worthiness of love and affection. They may also fear being judged or rejected—or may constantly compare themselves to others. These negative beliefs and insecurities can hinder the development of healthy and fulfilling connections, leading to emotional distance, avoidance, or self-sabotaging behaviors. If you've experienced negative aspects of yourself in previous relationships and you find yourself being triggered in your current relationship, you might find yourself questioning whether you've truly done the work to remedy your own issues. Being judgmental of yourself and expecting perfection in your new relationship can stand in the way of truly enjoying the company of the person that you're with.

This is why overcoming self-doubt and imposter syndrome in personal relationships requires a deep understanding of oneself and the courage to challenge negative thought patterns. By developing self-compassion and addressing these internal struggles, individuals can create stronger and more authentic connections with their loved ones, thus leading to greater fulfillment and emotional well-being.

However, if your work-related imposter syndrome is starting to affect your relationship and the above scenario is not true for you, there is still a fair amount of groundwork in the area of self-awareness that you can and should do.

Throughout this chapter, we will explore the impact of self-doubt and imposter syndrome on personal relationships. By recognizing the underlying causes and patterns, individuals can take proactive steps to build self-confidence, enhance communication skills, and foster healthier relationships. As we embark on this chapter, it is crucial to approach the exploration of personal relationships with an open mind and a willingness to delve into the vulnerable aspects of your life. By doing so, you'll be in a position to unravel the layers of self-doubt and imposter syndrome that hinder your personal connections.

From there, you can unlock the potential for more profound and meaningful relationships.

Imposter Syndrome in the Personal Realm

We've already briefly discussed this, but it's important to look at it in greater detail now. Self-doubt and imposter syndrome not only impact our professional lives but also have the potential to seep into our personal relationships, affecting our overall well-being and connections with others. The negative beliefs and self-perceptions that accompany these experiences can manifest in various ways, thus influencing the dynamics and quality of our relationships—and this applies to platonic relationships too!

One way self-doubt and imposter syndrome can affect personal relationships is through a constant need for validation and reassurance. When we doubt our abilities and worth, we may seek constant validation from our partners, friends, and family members. We may question their love, support, and loyalty, believing that we are not deserving of their affection. This can create a cycle of seeking reassurance and relying heavily on others' opinions to feel validated, which can strain relationships and create an emotional burden for both parties.

This, despite what you might think, is not necessarily because you come off as "needy" because that would imply that your needs don't matter. However, it can be incredibly burdensome for the people you love to watch you toil with your emotions and feel like they can't do anything except validate you to make you feel better. While relationships are worth fighting for, there is no guarantee that the people in your life have worked on themselves in the psychological aspects of their own lives. To assume that they do not have problems of their own and that they, therefore, can constantly carry the weight of your problems simply isn't fair. Any relationship that can be considered healthy involves two people who are committed to being the very best versions of themselves—primarily for themselves but for their partners too.

Add to this the fact that self-doubt and imposter syndrome can lead to a fear of vulnerability and intimacy, and we have a person who needs constant validation and who cannot reciprocate their partner's love language or fulfill their needs. In a relationship, imposter syndrome may cause the affected party to hesitate when it comes to opening up and sharing their true selves with others. If you're in a mental framework where you fear that opening up to your partner will expose you as a fraud, they will never understand why you have a constant need for validation. They will never understand your insecurity and will, therefore, never be able to support you on your path to building your self-confidence. This fear can hinder the development of deep and meaningful connections because you may hold back your authentic thoughts, feelings, and experiences. This will only create distance and barriers in your relationships.

Furthermore, self-doubt and imposter syndrome can contribute to a sense of unworthiness and comparison in personal relationships. Individuals may constantly compare themselves to their friends' other friends or their current partner's past partners. This mindset can lead to jealousy, insecurity, and resentment because they perceive themselves as inferior to others and struggle to embrace the moment within the relationship. Ultimately, these people will live inside their heads, cooking up scenarios that hurt their own feelings, and in some cases, they will bring certain scenarios into reality in an unconscious bid to fulfill their own worst fears.

This inability to receive and accept love and support from others will have you rejecting gestures of kindness, attributing them to mere pity or obligation. To cut a long story short, you may struggle to trust that others truly care for you.

To mitigate the impact of self-doubt and imposter syndrome on your personal relationships, it is crucial for you to engage in self-care practices. By developing a healthy sense of self-worth and embracing your authentic self, you can foster stronger connections with others. Seeking support from a therapist may be in order as they can provide a safe space for you to explore and address these challenges.

Learning how to share your fears, insecurities, and experiences of self-doubt can foster understanding and empathy, helping to build stronger bonds based on mutual support and acceptance. Similarly, engaging in activities that nurture your self-esteem and confidence, such as pursuing hobbies and setting personal goals, can also contribute to a healthier mindset and more fulfilling relationships.

Whatever you do, do not cling to one another harder in the moments when you're experiencing this level of imposter syndrome. What will bring you closer to one another is a healthy ability to focus on yourselves, your hobbies, and your personal pursuits. Clinging will create an unhealthy codependency that will almost guarantee the souring of your relationship. Develop strong identities outside of one another and allow your meeting in the middle to help your relationship thrive. This isn't to say that you should be cold and aloof with one another or that you should avoid spending time with one another. On the contrary, this means being so focused on your own goals and ambitions that you make the most of every precious moment with your partner.

Ultimately, by recognizing and addressing the impact of self-doubt and imposter syndrome on your personal relationships, you can cultivate healthier connections, foster deeper intimacy, and create a supportive network of individuals who value and appreciate you for who you truly are. This is not your sign to begin self-isolating. In fact, it's one of the worst things that you can do if it goes unchecked for a prolonged period of time.

Remember, it's always best to have supportive souls around.

Coming Back to Those Who Care

Imposter syndrome can cause you to withdraw from your loved ones. The feelings of inadequacy, the fear of being exposed, and the crippling self-doubt can lead to a sense of isolation and detachment.

OVERCOMING SELF-DOUBT AND IMPOSTER SYNDROME IN PERSONAL RELATIONSHIPS

This can create a barrier between yourself and the people who care about you. However, it is crucial for you to recognize the importance of reconnecting with loved ones and how sharing your experiences can restore and strengthen these relationships.

If you believe that by distancing yourself, you can protect others from discovering your perceived inadequacies, you're wrong. This withdrawal will only make you feel worse about past hurdles and current challenges. Withdrawal, if you're unaware, can manifest as a reluctance to engage in social activities. You'll find yourself declining invitations or limiting communication with friends and family. As a result, you may feel increasingly isolated and disconnected from your support network, thus exacerbating your feelings of self-doubt.

Reconnecting with loved ones is vital for several reasons. First, it provides a source of emotional support and understanding. Your loved ones can offer reassurance, empathy, and perspective, reminding you of your value and capabilities. They can help you challenge your negative self-perceptions and remind you of your achievements and strengths.

Second, rebuilding connections with loved ones can serve as a reality check. Often, your loved ones have a more accurate and objective perception of your abilities and accomplishments. Their perspective can help counter the distorted self-image created by imposter syndrome and remind you of the positive impact you have on their lives.

Essentially, explaining what you have gone through and why you became distant can be a cathartic and restorative process for everyone involved. Sharing your experiences of imposter syndrome with loved ones can foster empathy and understanding. It allows them to gain insight into the internal struggles you have been facing and helps them comprehend the reasons behind your withdrawal. This openness can deepen trust and create a safe space for vulnerability and authenticity within the relationship.

Moreover, explaining your journey with imposter syndrome can be empowering for you. It requires acknowledging your struggles and confronting your fears. By verbalizing your experiences, you take an important step toward reclaiming your authenticity and breaking the cycle of self-doubt and isolation. It allows you to redefine your narrative and move forward with greater self-acceptance and resilience.

In addition, the act of sharing can also encourage others who may be silently grappling with similar feelings of self-doubt and imposter syndrome. It opens the door for conversations about mental health and well-being, fostering a supportive environment where everyone can feel comfortable discussing their challenges and seeking help when needed. This can lead to healing and growth. It strengthens the bonds of trust and support, thus creating a foundation for more resilient relationships. It allows you to receive the love and acceptance you deserve and helps your loved ones understand and navigate the complexities of imposter syndrome.

It is important to approach these conversations with openness, vulnerability, and the intention to foster understanding. Active listening, empathy, and validation play crucial roles in these discussions. At the end of the day, what you want is to create a safe and non-judgmental space for everyone involved.

By reconnecting with loved ones and sharing your experiences, you can break free from the isolating grip of imposter syndrome, restore meaningful connections, and find solace in the collective support and understanding of those who care about you. Together, you can navigate the challenges of imposter syndrome and create a network of support that promotes growth, resilience, and well-being. To reconnect with your loved ones, try "Exercise 12: Reconnecting with Grace," which is available in your workbook.

From here, understanding the dynamics of how our society could be swaying you to act erratically and based on insecurity in your relationships is our next port of call.

The Reality of Our Global Society

In today's interconnected world, global issues such as body shaming, intellect shaming, and personal choice shaming have become increasingly prevalent. These societal pressures and judgments contribute to a culture of self-consciousness, where individuals constantly question their worth and abilities. This phenomenon is particularly relevant for leaders who are at the top of their professional game and often face additional scrutiny and expectations in their relationships. They can, therefore, become more susceptible to the pressures of our modern-day globalized society, and this can have detrimental effects on their self-esteem and confidence.

Society's emphasis on unrealistic beauty standards, for example, and the portrayal of "fitness" as an ideal can lead to body dissatisfaction and a sense of inadequacy. The constant scrutiny and judgment can contribute to feelings of self-consciousness and trigger imposter syndrome, where they doubt whether their partner or friends truly do care for them.

Similarly, personal choice shaming occurs when individuals face criticism or judgment for the decisions they make about their personal lives, such as career choices, relationships, or lifestyle preferences. People may experience personal choice shaming in various aspects of their lives, including their parenting choices, work-life balance, or unconventional career paths. These external judgments can create a sense of inadequacy and self-doubt, fueling imposter syndrome as they question their ability to make the right decisions and lead effectively.

The cumulative effect of these issues is a pervasive sense of self-consciousness that undermines one's confidence and fuels imposter syndrome. People may internalize societal expectations and judgments—constantly questioning their worth and qualifications in all aspects of life. They may believe that they need to meet impossible standards or suppress their authentic selves to gain acceptance and validation. As you can imagine, this is just as much a problem in one's personal relationships as it is in the workplace.

Addressing these issues requires a concerted effort to challenge the harmful narratives and judgments that perpetuate self-consciousness. Recognizing that external judgments do not define your worth and focusing on your unique strengths and contributions can help mitigate the impact of imposter syndrome in your personal life.

*

With the end of the penultimate chapter, we can begin looking into how you can maintain your self-confidence in the long run. This is going to be one of the most vital areas to work on because maintaining a change in your mindset and behavior is far harder than the change itself.

JB

CHAPTER 14

SUSTAINING CONFIDENCE OVER TIME

As you've made it to the end of our journey together, I strongly recommend taking the time to build the discipline to maintain what you've cultivated. Sustaining your confidence as a leader—whether you're a captain of international industry or leader of a local organization—is of the utmost importance at this stage.

As you know by now, confidence serves as a cornerstone for effective leadership—empowering you to make sound decisions, inspire your team, and navigate the challenges that come your way. It is an essential quality that not only influences your own mindset but also has a profound impact on those around you. When you exude confidence, you inspire trust. You also encourage collaboration and motivate others to believe in the collective vision along the way.

However, maintaining confidence as a leader is not a one-time accomplishment but an ongoing journey. It requires continuous effort, self-reflection, and adaptability. The world is in a constant state of change, and as a leader, you must stay attuned to the evolving landscape and adapt your leadership style accordingly. By remaining open to new ideas, embracing innovation, and embracing change, you can maintain your confidence and lead your team with conviction and agility.

Without further ado, let's explore your final subchapters on your road to becoming the self-confident leader that you and your team deserve.

Keeping Up Confidence in the Long Run

As a leader, maintaining confidence during challenging times and setbacks is crucial for resilience and continued growth. You will eventually reach an obstacle on your journey. In fact, leadership roles are born of the need to have someone guiding a team as they traverse these tough challenges together. If there were never any problems to tackle, leaders would be redundant. Everyone would just get on with their respective roles without ever worrying about a single thing going awry. While setbacks are a natural part of any leadership journey, they can sometimes shake our confidence and trigger self-doubt. However, with the right strategies, we can navigate these difficulties and emerge stronger than ever.

Now, you might be thinking that you already know how to tackle self-doubt—after all, that is what this entire book has been about. However, this subchapter isn't going to look into navigating self-doubt but rather will explore keeping up your confidence in the long run.

First and foremost, it is essential to cultivate the habit of keeping up good habits. How solid and committed you are regarding your habits will determine whether you're sitting on a life raft or a yacht during storms—those that occur both in your life and in your organization. Here's why. When you're already so accustomed to completing your daily habits, they will be second nature to you. Your habits will land somewhere between breathing and brushing your teeth in terms of how consistently and effortlessly they come to you, even in times of trouble. If you can commit to your habits and realize that they are elements of your day that work for your greater good, you will maintain your self-confidence throughout every season. Be aware that this doesn't necessarily mean that you're going to feel like you're oozing confidence during tough times as a result of your habits, but they will act as a stopper—preventing your self-confidence from yo-yoing. What's more, it's easier to bounce back emotionally when you're only dealing with a setback as opposed to dealing with a setback **and** having to pick up the slack from dropped habits.

Adopting the mindset of a lifelong learner will do you tons of good in maintaining your self-confidence and assuring that it stems from within rather than from the validation of other people. When you're constantly reading up on your industry and learning more about the evolution of your specific role on a global level, no one can make you feel as though you're not abreast of what's current. Feelings of ineptitude and lack of authority in your field cannot wrestle as strongly with your mind if your mind is steeped in current trends and information regarding your career, role, and industry.

Teach yourself how to engage in constructive self-reflection rather than dwelling on self-criticism, and do so while you're in a favorable season. Practicing in the good times is just as important as learning from experience in the tough times. This is why athletes practice for months at a time to play one game or attend one event. You can't just walk headfirst into the moment and know what to do with it without practicing first. To engage in self-reflection, make a habit out of analyzing all situations objectively. Try to see everything as outside of yourself and not as a part of your identity. This will allow you to rapidly identify any areas for improvement and develop an action plan to address them. When you embrace this mindset of continuous learning and growth, maintaining a stable and constant level of self-confidence will be far easier. And this is truly the key here. It's not about having insanely high levels of self-confidence. That isn't the answer to beating imposter syndrome. It's all about maintaining a level that feels suitable to you and avoiding rampant spikes.

Don't try to go too hard in too many different directions. Maintain a manageable stability everywhere instead, including in your professional life and relationships. When you have a moment, engage in self-reflection using "Exercise 13: Engaging in Objective Analysis."

When you're on the level with yourself, delving into the type of relationships you're maintaining and how they help (or hinder) your self-confidence will be up next.

Growing & Nurturing Your Network

So, you know how to find mentors and build a support network, but do you know how to nurture those connections? Nurturing a supportive network of mentors, sponsors, and peers is essential for personal and professional growth as a leader. These individuals can provide guidance, advice, and valuable insights while also serving as a source of encouragement and support. Building and maintaining such a network requires intentional effort and a proactive approach.

You have to be incredibly clear about your goals and areas where you would benefit from guidance or support. Be clear about what you hope to achieve and the specific areas where you believe mentors, sponsors, or peers can provide valuable input. This is important for a number of reasons, but one of them is that you should be able to speak about the type of support that you need. When you're unclear on why you want a mentor and what you want to gain out of your support network, it's impossible to receive those gifts from the people around you. Just try to remain cognizant of the mindset that you have to give before you can receive. Your priority should always be to provide value to your network. Not only will this help you maintain your level of confidence, but it will also give you the ability to ask for support when you actually need it. Finding genuine satisfaction in serving others will also boost your leadership abilities as you learn to give for the betterment of others and not just for the promise of future reward.

When it comes to maintaining these relationships with mentors or sponsors, be respectful and considerate of their time and commitments. If someone has gone out of their way to dedicate time to your growth and development, be mindful of this. There are many things that we can get back in life, but time is not one of them. More importantly, recognize that your mentor sees something worth spending time on when they look at you and your trajectory. Speaking of your trajectory, you could consider surrounding yourself with individuals who are on a similar leadership journey or who are facing similar challenges. Forming peer relationships allows for mutual support, collaboration, and the opportunity to share insights as well as resources. Just remember, the key is to give more than you receive. It is important to reciprocate and contribute to the relationship by offering your own insights, support, and encouragement when appropriate. Share your own experiences, perspectives, and expertise in order to demonstrate that you value the mutual exchange of knowledge and support.

Ultimately, nurturing a supportive network requires ongoing effort and investment. Be proactive in seeking feedback, advice, and opportunities for growth. Actively participate in professional development activities, such as workshops, conferences, or training programs, where you can expand your network and engage with like-minded individuals. This will strengthen your confidence as you learn more about your industry and your role from people who have gone before you—and don't forget to bounce ideas off those who are currently on a similar journey beside you.

Then, you can focus on your adaptability.

Driving Adaptability

Building a routine and having habits that ensure your stability is vital to any leader's success, but so is adaptability. Nurturing resilience and adapting to change are crucial in any high-pressure career. In a dynamic and fast-paced work environment, challenges and unexpected situations are inevitable. By embracing change as a constant factor, you empower yourself to navigate the ever-evolving professional landscape with confidence.

That is why understanding that change is the only constant, as previously mentioned, is fundamental to your ability to adapt. Rather than resisting or fearing change, embrace it as an opportunity for growth and improvement. View change as a chance to explore new avenues, challenge yourself, and broaden your horizons. In today's fast-paced world, this is needed as a precursor to the ability to adapt quickly. Staying nimble and flexible in your approach keeps you in a position of readiness to adjust your strategies, processes, and mindset as circumstances demand. Adaptability enables you to respond effectively to unexpected challenges and seize new opportunities.

If you truly want to embrace the human ability to adapt, commit to being open to new ideas and perspectives no matter what your personal circumstances. Encourage collaboration and diverse thinking in your team by encouraging them to seek out opinions and feedback from colleagues, mentors, and industry experts. Then, show them how it's done! Embracing different viewpoints will always lead to innovative solutions and an expansion of your own understanding. To become more adaptable in your approach, consider "Exercise 14: Enhancing Adaptability," which can be found in your workbook.

With a few tools for becoming more adaptable, you can turn to the 4 Cs of Adaptability [9], which are concern, control, curiosity, and confidence. Concern involves looking toward the future and planning ahead. Control refers to how much control you're able to exercise over your career trajectory through your self-discipline and conscious efforts to stay abreast of changes. Curiosity is centered around dreaming, visualizing, and then manifesting your aspirations. Finally, confidence—as we're currently exploring—is rooted in your sense of self-efficacy. If you have high levels of each of the 4 Cs, you'll be more adaptable in your career, and this in itself can keep you confident in your abilities.

This, in turn, will drive continual growth.

Continuing Your Growth

Continuing to grow and develop as a confident leader requires a multifaceted approach that goes beyond some of the strategies mentioned before. The first of these final strategies involves taking a different stance with regard to mentorship. Whereas you will have sought guidance before, you can now begin offering guidance to others. You'll know that it is time to do this when you're feeling stable and capable enough in your own abilities to begin sharing your insight and expertise.

Sharing your knowledge and experiences by mentoring and supporting aspiring leaders in your field will be a great way to pay it forward. This is also a surefire way to keep yourself grounded and grateful for the journey that you have been on, as well as the road that still lies ahead of you. It will serve as a reminder of your own hardships and reinforce the strength that it took for you to overcome them. As you share these insights with mentees, their struggles (perhaps even with imposter syndrome) will provide you with renewed insight into the phenomena, keeping you confident and providing support to those who need it most. By offering guidance, advice, and encouragement to help others overcome their self-doubt and imposter syndrome, you will keep your own at bay. Therefore, try to engage in initiatives that promote diversity and inclusivity in leadership and advocate for equal opportunities.

Remember, growth and development as a confident leader is an ongoing process. Embrace the journey with curiosity, resilience, and a commitment to continuous improvement. By harnessing your strengths, seeking support, and embracing new challenges, you can navigate the complexities of leadership and make a lasting impact.

*

Stumbling and falling are expected, so be kind and loving. Give yourself grace as you continue to grow and improve. And remember, we will no longer overdose on doubt. We will overcome it.

Your next is right now!

JB

CONCLUSION
CALL TO ACTION

As we've progressed, I hope you've taken particular note of the various manifestations of self-doubt and imposter syndrome. This will help you to identify the specific challenges associated with the phenomena.

It's important that you're able to build the self-awareness that will allow you to assess the type of imposter syndrome you're experiencing, as well as the means by which it can be recognized. Doing this will prime you for the steps that you'll need to take to overcome self-doubt and build your inner confidence.

Know that there are various leadership styles that you can pick from as you go about identifying the most suitable style for you and your team. Always remember that you are not bound to one specific leadership style for the rest of your life. In fact, some of the most notable leaders around the world have benefited from blended leadership styles—picking the optimal traits for each situation they find themselves navigating.

Developing the right skills to complement these leadership traits is imperative. Learning how to communicate your thoughts and inspire others to take action is a must for every leader. A team that is fully onboard with your objectives and goals for the organization will make the process of pinpointing bias and discrimination in the workplace far more direct. As you learn to navigate workplace bias and take claim of a positive, self-supporting inner voice, you'll find that tapping into the power of your vulnerability doesn't feel as threatening as it perhaps once did.

Ultimately, you'll be able to build and sustain your self-confidence over time.

This is crucial because the importance of modern-day transformational leadership cannot be overstated. By bringing diverse perspectives, skills, and experiences to the table, you can contribute to more inclusive decision-making processes and foster innovation within your organization. This has a ripple effect throughout our communities, cities, nations, and the world.

When we overcome imposter syndrome, we unlock our true potential and become powerful role models for others.

By sharing your stories and demonstrating resilience, you will inspire future generations to rise above self-doubt and pursue leadership positions. Furthermore, leaders who conquer imposter syndrome often create supportive environments that encourage their team members to thrive, thus fostering a culture of empowerment and growth.

To all readers, I urge you to continue implementing the strategies and exercises shared in this book and its accompanying workbook. Overcoming self-doubt and imposter syndrome

CALL TO ACTION

is a journey that requires consistent effort and commitment. Remember that change doesn't happen overnight, but with perseverance, you can conquer these challenges and unlock your true potential.

Embrace the power of self-reflection and self-awareness. Be vigilant in recognizing when self-doubt or imposter syndrome creeps in. Use the practical tools and exercises provided to challenge negative thoughts, practice self-compassion, and cultivate a growth mindset.

When all else seems to be faltering, surround yourself with a supportive network of mentors, peers, and allies who believe in your abilities. Seek guidance from those who have overcome similar challenges and draw inspiration from their stories.

Most importantly, be patient with (and kind to) yourself throughout this process. Remember that setbacks and doubts are natural, but they don't define you. You are capable of greatness.

Believe in your unique talents, embrace your strengths, and step into your leadership journey with confidence.

The world needs your voice and contributions.

JB

REFERENCES & CITATIONS

1. Hernandez, M., & Lacerenza, C. 2023. *How to Help High Achievers Overcome Imposter Syndrome.* MIT Sloan Management Review, 64(2), 1-5. https://www.proquest.com/openview/2a665cb7ff66b938547cf9c50d93eb6d/1?pq-origsite=gscholar&cbl=26142
2. Zourbanos, N., et al. 2011. *The social side of self-talk: Relationships between perceptions of support received from the coach and athletes' self-talk.* Psychology of Sport and Exercise. Volume 12, Issue 4, July 2011, Pages 407-414. https://doi.org/10.1016/j.psychsport.2011.03.001
3. Demarin, V. i MOROVIĆ, S. 2014. *Neuroplasticity.* Periodicum biologorum, 116 (2), 209-211. Preuzeto s https://hrcak.srce.hr/126369
4. World Bank Team. 2022. *Nearly 2.4 Billion Women Globally Don't Have Same Economic Rights as Men.* The World Bank. https://www.worldbank.org/en/news/press-release/2022/03/01/nearly-2-4-billion-women-globally-don-t-have-same-economic-rights-as-men
5. Weisberg, Y. J., DeYoung, C. G., & Hirsh, J. B. 2011. *Gender Differences in Personality across the Ten Aspects of the Big Five.* Frontiers in Psychology, 2, 178. https://doi.org/10.3389/fpsyg.2011.00178

REFERENCES & CITATIONS

6. White, D. G. 1985. *Ar'n't I a Woman?: Female Slaves in the Plantation South*. New York, New York. W. W. Norton and Company Inc.
7. Brown, B. 2018. *Dare to Lead: Brave Work. Tough Conversations. Whole Hearts.* New York, New York. Penguin Random House,
8. Williams, S. 2022. *How Serena Williams Saved Her Own Life*. Elle. https://www.elle.com/life-love/a39586444/how-serena-williams-saved-her-own-life/
9. Neureiter, Mirjam., Traut-Mattausch, Eva. 2017. *Two sides of the career resources coin: Career adaptability resources and the impostor phenomenon.* Journal of Vocational Behavior, Volume 98. https://doi.org/10.1016/j.jvb.2016.10.002.

JB